HYPNEROTOMACHIA POLIPHILI

* * *

* *

*

HYPNEROTOMACHIA POLIPHILI

RE-DISCOVERING ANTIQUITY
THROUGH THE DREAMS OF POLIPHILUS

ESTEBAN ALEJANDRO CRUZ

*Artist reconstructions of the architecture and landscapes
described by Poliphilus during his amorous quest
through 'Antiquity'*

Note for Librarians: A cataloguing record for this book is available from
Library and Archives Canada at www.collectionscanada.ca/amicus/index-e.html
ISBN 1-4120-5324-2

Printed in Victoria, BC, Canada. Printed on paper with minimum 30% recycled fibre.
Trafford's print shop runs on "green energy" from solar, wind and other environmentally-friendly power sources.

Offices in Canada, USA, Ireland and UK

Book sales for North America and international:
Trafford Publishing, 6E–2333 Government St.,
Victoria, BC V8T 4P4 CANADA
phone 250 383 6864 (toll-free 1 888 232 4444)
fax 250 383 6804; email to orders@trafford.com
Book sales in Europe:
Trafford Publishing (UK) Limited, 9 Park End Street, 2nd Floor
Oxford, UK OX1 1HH UNITED KINGDOM
phone 44 (0)1865 722 113 (local rate 0845 230 9601)
facsimile 44 (0)1865 722 868; info.uk@trafford.com
Order online at:
trafford.com/05-0219

10 9 8 7 6 5 4 3 2

CONTENTS

*

NOTA BENE: With the exceptions of N°6 , 14, 19, 21, 23, 31,43, and 44, all illustrations listed here in the text section of this book, are original woodcuts* from the *Hypnerotomachia.*

* Woodcuts from Francesco Colonna, *Hypnerotomachia Poliphili: The strife of Love in a Dream*, translated by Joscelyn Godwin, Thames & Hudson, London and New York.
Woodcuts from Francesco Colonna, *Le Songe de Poliphile*, translated by Jean Martin (Paris, Kerver 1546), Imprimerie Nationale Éditions, Paris.

I

ILLUSTRATIONS

*

PLATES

*

PLATES

*

PLATES

*

ACKNOWLEDGEMENTS

*

My involvement with the *Hypnerotomachia Poliphili* has been a 12 year project, and for this reason I would like to acknowledge the help and guidance of a few colleagues and institutions; without their contribution in one way or another, this book would not have been possible. Firstly, my thanks goes to Ferdinando Lugli of *Centro Ricerche S.c.a.r.l.*, Carpi (Modena) for his mentoring in methodology, history and computers during my collaborations with his company. This work, without a doubt, was only possible with his valuable scientific guidance on methodologies.

I would like to thank Dr. Stefano Colonna of the *Festina Lente* Research Institute (CIRSA-Roma), and Prof. Maurizio Calvesi of the University of Rome. Their critiques and scientific appreciation for my work were quite encouraging during the later years of this project. I cannot leave out an additional appreciation to Dr. Colonna for having invited me to present samples of this project at a book conference in Rome last year, which involved the participation of Prof. Calvesi, Stefano Borsi, and other scholars whose works were also helpful for this project's development.

The genesis of this work during the first years of its development benefited from the following people: Bilgi Denel of the California Polytechnic State University (San Luis Obispo) for his inspiring lectures on the importance of the poetry of architecture and the vernacular; conversations and critiques with Giuseppe Tore Frulio of the University of Alghero (Sardinia) regarding historic preservation and ancient building methods; Cristiano Toraldo di Francia of the California State University Florence for his discussions on architecture and archetypes; the *Biblioteca Estense di Modena* for their valuable help with historic documents and bibliography; the *Archivio Storico di Verona* for their assistance in allowing me to study their original Aldine copy of the *Hypnerotomachia*. During the later part of this work, Marino Zancanella of the University of Parma invited me to give a presentation at one of his lectures on design. His interest and critical feedback were very helpful during the completion of the work's final layout.

This book could not have been possible without the assistance and resources of the following individuals: Marco Papotti, of INTECO Engineering (Mantua) for graciously granting use of their computer graphics & plotting facilities; Cristiano Alberti of Grafikando (Varese) for their rendering services. An infinite recognition goes to Ellen Singer (San Diego) for her valuable writing consultations and editing.

My gratitude also goes to Silvia Fogliati and Davide Dutto, for their critiques and interest in my work on the *Hypnerotomachia*. A special thanks goes to Silvia for her kind hospitality and for having encouraged me to pursue my work.

I cannot thank Piero Meogrossi of the *Sovrintendenza Archeologica del Colosseo* and Stella Pedana in Rome, more than enough for their mutual interest in my reconstructions, as well as their valuable feedback during this on-going project. Perusing with Piero and Stella through unknown corners of the Palatine Hill, while discovering secrets and significance of Roman Antiquity was quite informative beyond the mere library hall.

HYPNEROTOMACHIA POLIPHILI:

RE-DISCOVERING ANTIQUITY THROUGH

THE DREAMS OF POLIPHILUS

*   *   *

*   *

*

INTRODUCTION

*

FORMAS IMAGINISQUE POLIPHILI:

Toward a Graphical Understanding of the *Hypnerotomachia*

Five hundred years ago, an operatic tale of unrequited love and female erotica, launched a more available and sustaining passion in Renaissance architecture. What has remained inaccessible, however, is a complete understanding of the *Hypnerotomachia Poliphili,* the text and haunting woodcuts that fascinated European civilization upon its publication in Venice in 1499, inspiring artists, architects, and patrons ever since.

The importance of the image has always been a fundamental aspect of iconographic, human communication, and it is the vivid imagery described by the dreamer in search of his lost love and the introduction of more than 160 beautifully, haunting illustrations that has made *Hypnerotomachia Poliphili* as fascinating today as it was in the late fifteenth century when the Press of Aldus Manutius first published this graphically exquisite book.

The story of Poliphilus, whose lust for the indifferent Polia is rivaled only by the carnal pleasures he encounters in the incredible architecture, gardens, and landscapes of his sleeping imaginations, has inspired centuries of architects to create similar sensuality in the smoothness of marble or curvature of arch in the real-life buildings they designed[1].

The cryptic messages, fantastic architecture, innovative graphic designs and layouts of the *Hypnerotomachia Poliphili* have moved and stirred western culture, prompting translators then and now to seek richer understanding of the author's (or authors') intent. It remains uncertain who wrote the book, but the writer – singular or plural -- seemed to want to produce a very spatial and graphic architectural treatise[2].

This text was too visionary for its time, and it was published during a crucial turning point in history. The late 1400s in Rome were not very safe for the intellectually and scientifically curious. Renaissance academies that once flourished under the court of Nicholas V became underground collegiate societies dispersed under the following rule of the Borgia Papacy. The *Hypnerotomachia Poliphili* was itself discreetly published in Venice, which at that time was an attractive city for its innovative interests and developments, far away from the Papal States. Although I am not attempting to argue as to who wrote the original manuscript, one couldn't help as to suggest that it was a group effort, an innovative way of working together that truly expresses the renaissance and humanist spirit of its time.

Since the *Hypnerotomachia* came about within this context, the visions and wonders described in the original Aldine manuscript are presented in an overwhelming play of philological and archeological allegories. In order to have a better understanding of what this visionary *incunabulum* contains, I am, with my project, proposing to use graphical and architectural forms of critical analysis instead of literary studies traditionally associated with scholarly work in the past (whose works I mention in the first chapter "methods"). For this reason, I am proposing: *Formas Imaginisque Poliphili,* which means "imaginary models of Poliphilus" revealed.

My Contribution to the Study of *Hypnerotomachia Poliphili*

By utilizing the technology of today with the history and traditions of the past, I hoped to develop a first series of digital, artist reconstructions of the architecture and landscapes described in this enigmatic book of the early renaissance. Since I was dealing with building and environmental design, the passages were quite familiar to those of a basic design background: research, vignettes, scale-measurement-proportion, practical simulations, etc., while at the same time, employing experience and methods developed during my previous work with re-constructing historic Bologna.[3] In addition to this, literary resources such as the works of Leon Battista Alberti, as well as the works of contemporary experts, were reconsidered in order to arrive at a critical and regional development of architectural vocabulary needed to realize these artist reconstructions.

In the end, my artwork of Poliphilus' architecture and insight into its significance within the Antiquarian context are presented here as an attempt to share an added deciphering of this labyrinthine text, bringing to life and giving significance to its fantastic architecture and allegorical visions.

With this in mind, I invite you now to witness the visions of a 500 year old dream of sublime beauty, ferocity, liberty, grace, and most important: Love.

E.A.C.

Milan, 2006

Chapter One

Methods & Challenges
in Visual Interpretation

1. POLIPHILUS & POLIA ARRIVE AT AN ANCIENT PORT

THIS BOOK IS AN ATTEMPT TO ILLUSTRATE WHAT BEFORE WAS almost impossible to see without surviving the *Hypnerotomachia*'s exhaustive language. My aim is to bring the text alive with artist reconstructions, to *show* what Poliphilus describes in his dream account, where descriptions of architecture are often lost on the readers of the almost incomprehensible passages.   Much of the value of the *Hypnerotomachia*'s (and certainly much of its beauty) is diminished by the author's labyrinthine and encyclopaedic way of using language.   My goal is to increase the significance of the work through an artistic rather than textual interpretation. With a few exceptions, *nothing like this has ever been accomplished at a large scale* (that is, toward reconstructing a complete set of monuments described by Poliphilus). Historically, only one artist had attempted even a limited reconstruction. The works of Eustache Le Sueur, (1617-1655) include a few paintings depicting Poliphilus' visions and experiences.[1] And only recently has a colleague of mine, Silvia Fogliati, been able to attempt a virtual reconstruction of the Island of Citera according to Poliphilus (published by Franco Maria Ricci)[2]

This work is not an attempt to find the "truth" behind this renaissance text, nor is it a disrespectful imposition on literary traditions associated with this scholarly work. I invite readers to make their own such judgments. Instead, these reconstructions were a result of trying to understand the *Hypnerotomachia* along with its difficult language.

*   *   *

*   *

*

METHODOLOGY: A BRIEF DESCRIPTION OF METHODS UTILIZED IN DEVELOPING THE ARTIST, VIRTUAL RECONSTRUCTIONS

The work began with a rigorous and critical reading of the original Aldine text. I took note of every detail describing ornament, architecture, measurement, and construction. At first I made sketches directly onto the pages of the contemporary Italian translations as a way of understanding Poliphilus' descriptions. Naturally, the page margins did not provide enough space for this practice, so I moved to a sketch book, where I attempted to piece together the architectural clues left behind by this 500-year-old narrator, to at least "picture" what he was describing. The way the text originally presented itself, even after its modern translation, made it almost impossible for me to envision his dream with clarity. Both the language and the encyclopaedic presentation used by the author made my goal difficult.

Still, sketching was a necessary step to get something out of what the author had encrypted in his pseudo-invented language. (The text is written mostly in Italian, but is full of words coined from Latin and Greek roots, as well as words from Arabic, Greek, Hebrew and hieroglyphic languages[3]. And when these languages didn't suffice, the author invented his own.) After a few conclusions on drawing form, literary research was necessary in order to understand significance of the classical samples that were introduced by the author. Almost for each monument, I had to create a "database" of information in order to keep up with Poliphilus while describing materials of construction, ornamentation, archetypes, et cetera. I constantly updated my sketches[4].

Simultaneously, I examined contemporary works by important scholars in the field of the *Hypnerotomachia* and early Renaissance Humanism in order to understand the significance and context of what I was producing in my sketchbooks: the works of

Professor Maurizio Calvesi[5], Emanuela Kretzulesco-Quaranta[6], Liane Lefaivre[7], Stefano Borsi[8], translations and comments by G. Pozzi, L.A. Ciapponi[9], Marco Ariani, Mino Gabriele[10], and Pilar Pedraza[11]. The classics where also very helpful: Leon Battista Alberti[12] and Vitruvius[13]. The best resource was the original *Hypnerotomachia Poliphili* itself. I also studied the 1546 French edition translated by Jean Martin[14], as well as the first, partial English translation by Robert Dallington in 1592[15]. Although my research and graphic work started many years before its publication, the first, complete English translation by Joscelyn Godwin[16] in 1999 was a pleasant help to the linguistic challenges I had to face.

Through the years while on study and practice assignments, traveling through the Veneto and the Lazio regions of Italy helped me in my research. I had begun collecting images and composing drawings of architectural works and techniques that seemed related to what I was finally "releasing" from the *Hypnerotomachia* with my sketches. In the end, while sorting all the evidence both from the text and from what I was collecting from my travels, I allowed computer graphics to assist me in doing the rest.

The resulting virtual reconstructions are not by all means perfect renditions of Poliphilus' words nor are they technologically perfect compared to what can be done with a professional computer animator or modeler. Instead, it is at least a first attempt to visualize those gardens, palaces, and architectural masterpieces, which have inspired theorists and practitioners over the centuries, encrypted in an almost unreadable mechanism of allegories.

Regardless to say, this project is ongoing. Monuments that I have attempted to piece together are still missing vital components within their computer graphic renditions. There are still many aspects described by Poliphilus that have not been included in these reconstructions partly for technological limitations and partly because they are still subject to study and design.

2. POLIPHILUS AMONGST ANCIENT RUINS (FRENCH EDITION)

VISIONARY VS. ANTIQUE:

Among my challenges in visual interpretation was to distinguish "antique" from "visionary" according to Poliphilus. While describing "classical" ruins, it was not difficult identifying images similar to those in Piranesi's etchings two hundred years later while illustrating Roman antiquity. In this case, research was involved in trying to design based on what the early humanists must have observed while surrounded by antiquity in the only place where legend and a strong classical past intertwine: Rome. Examples of temples, grand arches, baths, and much more, consumed by time and the disgrace of pillage, were plentiful. At the same time, Rome was a site of study and interest on the part of the early renaissance humanists including Pomponio Leto and others whose platonic ideals and love of the antique helped form a true antiquarian society. Poliphilus himself shared his interest and admiration for the technological beauty of the architecture built by the ancients as a sign of great wisdom long forgotten[17] while despising his contemporary architects for their ignorance[18].

On the other hand, Poliphilus also mentions certain buildings that imply a new architecture[19] that reveals itself only in the century following the publication of the *Hypnerotomachia Poliphili*. The best example is his description of the Palace of Queen Eleutirillide.[20] With extravagant, almost baroque use of decoration, he describes its interiors with few clues and gives only a hint as to its exterior composition. He mentions a symmetrical plan with an orderly distribution of rooms, courtyard spaces, highly decorated walls with frescoes, articulate wood coffer ceilings decorated in gold, two hundred columns[21], marble sculpture and ornamentation. With seeming awe, Poliphilus presents the reader with this list as if it was impossible to describe in totality the palace's massive composition as he had done successfully with the temple to Venus Physizoa. In fact, the author dedicates more time to describing the labyrinthine parks and gardens adjacent to the Queen's palace.

Based on Poliphilus' indications, the plan for the palace was not difficult for me to reconstruct. However, the challenge came to "designing" its exterior architecture or façades. Most design choices start with a strong concept. The *Hypnerotomachia Poliphili* was published on a date that was a turning point in European civilization. A new hemisphere had been discovered and political changes were rebalancing the power struggle in Europe, giving birth to new, modern states. Architecture was a consequence to these events and the *Hypnerotomachia* as a genre was a perfect mixture between late medieval literary traditions and a new innovative consciousness typical of the late *Quattrocento*[22]. It was a perfect symbol of the changing times and transformations from a late medieval society to a modern area. For this reason, I chose to examine samples of the second Renaissance, that is, the *Cinquecento*, as an inspiration in developing motifs for the reconstruction of Queen Eleutirillide's palace due to the fact that Poliphilus hints to forms that are not typical of his period[23]. It seemed appropriate to choose a more mature form of architectural history since the *Cinquecento* was an implementation and further development of what was previously initiated by the efforts of theorists such as Alberti, Filarete, and especially Francesco di Giorgio in the century before[24]. In fact, the works of Sebastiano Serlio[25] and the architecture of the period were very helpful in initiating concepts for decorations, planning issues, and architectural conception.

There were also challenges in visual interpretation, especially discrepancy with the amount of detail of Poliphilus' descriptions in his dream. In some cases, the author dedicates many pages with minute details and artistic description to one monument and its parts, leaving little space for interpretation as in the case of the Temple to Venus *Physizoa*. In other parts of the *Hypnerotomachia*, and in the case of the Polyandrion of Lost Loves, for example, Poliphilus alludes to only certain archetypes and materials, without describing in detail the rest. This leaves the reader perplexed as to how its architecture was composed (or de-composed.) In these cases, it was as if I had to assume the role of archaeologist in piecing together a "history" of monuments with only those clues left behind while excavating into the depths of the *Hypnerotomachia.* Poliphilus left room for interpretation, so I had to study and "design" the rest.

This leads to possible complications between erudite imagination and complete fantasy even to Poliphilus. Thanks to the aid of generations of scholarly research and bibliography as a guide, I hoped to have created images that are close to an honest reconstruction as can be accomplished. Once again, this is an ongoing project, which I hope will become of interest and further development. As the ancient inscription deciphered by Poliphilus suggests, if my patience is protection and life's décor, then most certainly I will continue to believe in this project with as much patience as possible.

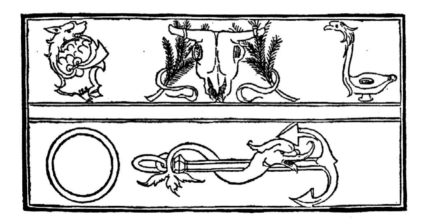

3. Patientia Est Ornamentum Custodia et Protectio Vitae

A NOTE ON ANCIENT MEASUREMENTS:

Almost all measurement terms utilized in the *Hypnerotomachia* refer to an order of standards used during ancient Roman times. The idea of a "standard," as we know of today, was quite different in those times; they were more like approximate "guidelines." Such standards where different depending in what part of the Empire you presented yourself in. If we choose, as an example, the quintessential Roman "foot" or *pes romanus*, you will notice that in Rome it was circa 29.7 cm. This was different than the *pes romanus* used in Pompei, which was about 27 cm (with a difference of 2.7 cm. circa). If this may seem insignificant, just imagine what the difference may have been when dividing large territorial spaces, such as farmland or property lots in different parts of the Empire!

Although the *pes romanus* was originally based on the Attic foot (not assuming however that the standards utilized in the Greek world could have coincided with those utilized throughout the Roman Empire), the actual "standard" was conserved in the temple of *Iuno Moneta* in Rome, similarly as we do today with our international Metric System in Paris.

Even after the fall of the Roman Empire, the same terms remained more or less in use, however the actual measurements changed from town to town in the Italian peninsula during the Middle Ages.

In order to have a better understanding of the "feel" or concept of space introduced in the *Hypnerotomachia*, the following multiples and sub-divisions of the Roman foot are presented here:

Roman term	Term utilized in HP-Godwin	Modern equivalent
pes	foot	29.65 cm.
sextan (*doran*) = 3/4 of a *pes*		
palmus = 1/4 of a *pes*	palm	7.41 cm.
uncia = 1/12 of a *pes*	inch	2.47 cm.
digitus = 1/16 of a *pes*		
cubitus = 1.5 *pes*	cubit	44.48 cm.
gradus = 2.5 *pes*		
passus = 5 *pes*	pace	1.49 meters
pertica = 10 *pes*		
actus = 120 *pes*		
stadium = 652 *pes*	stadium	193.32 meters
milium = 5000 *pes*	mile	1.49 kilometers

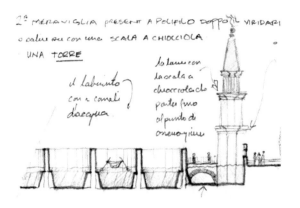

PLATES

METHODS *&* CHALLENGES
IN
VISUAL INTEPRETATION

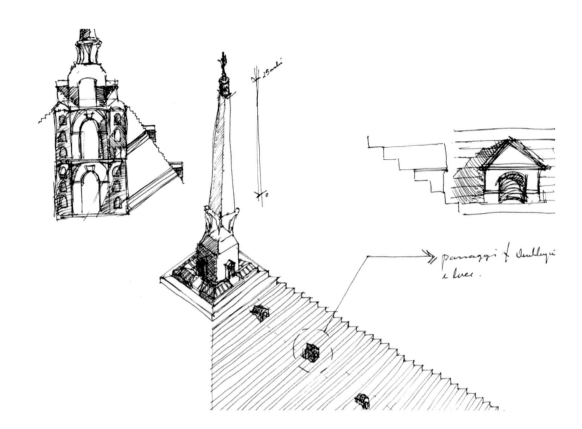

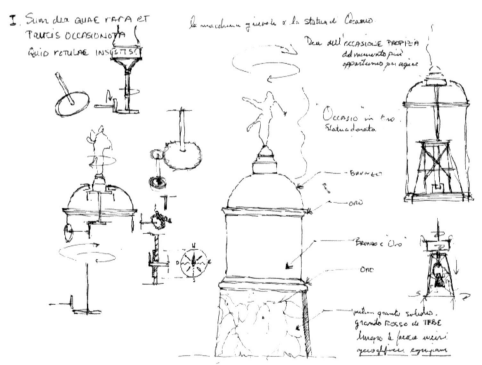

PLATE I

SKETCHES & SCHEMATICS FOR THE PYRAMID OF FORTUNE

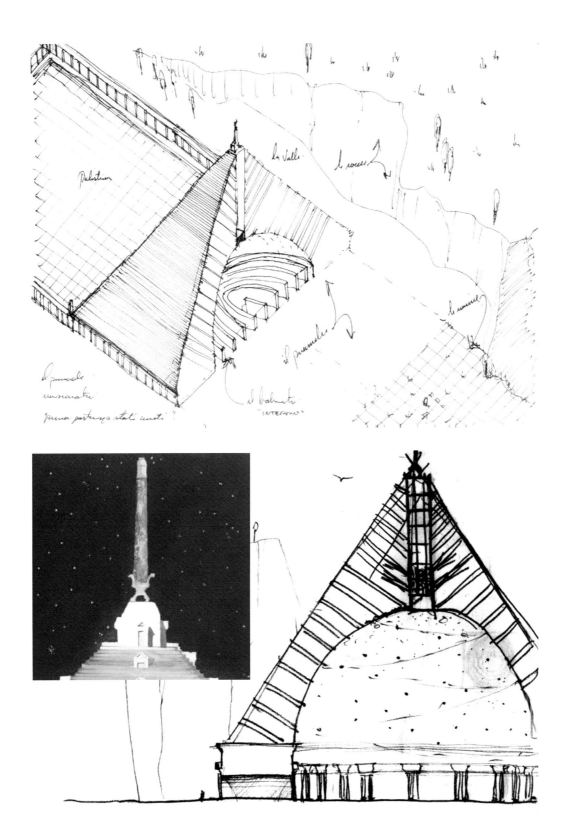

PLATE II

SKETCHES & SCHEMATICS FOR THE PYRAMID OF FORTUNE

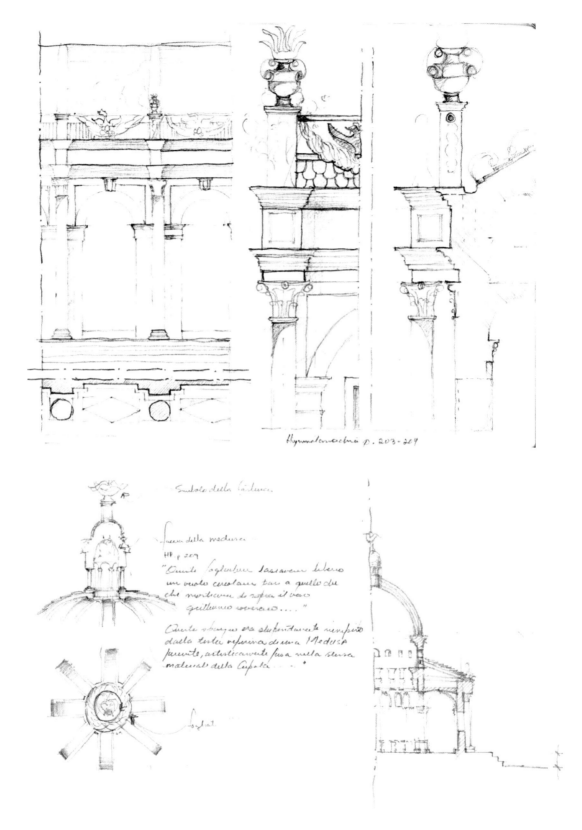

PLATE III

SKETCHES & SCHEMATICS FOR THE TEMPLE TO VENUS PHYSIZOA

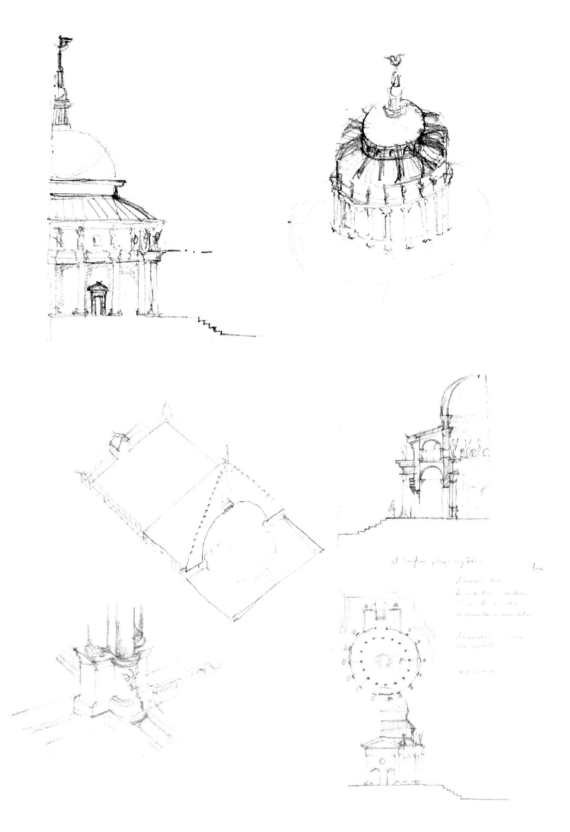

PLATE IV

SKETCHES & SCHEMATICS FOR THE TEMPLE TO VENUS PHYSIZOA

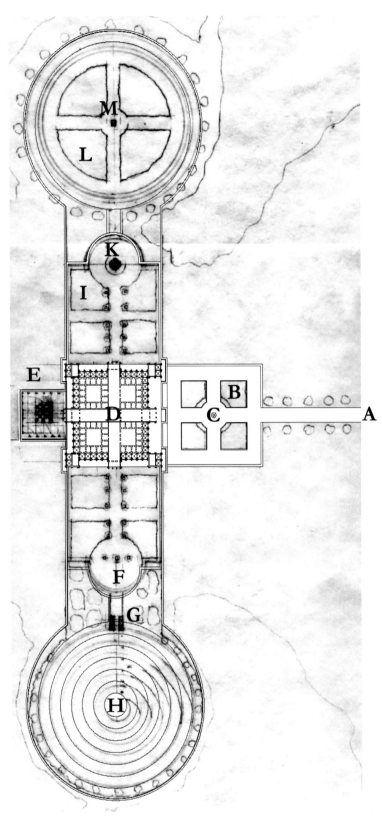

LEGEND

A *Entrance*

B *Main courtyard*

C *Fountain with the three nymphs*

D *Main palace complex with courtyards and porticoes*

E *Courtyard of the Queen's throne with representations of the celestial bodies*

F *Garden of Glass "Viridarium"*

G *Tower & entrance to the labyrinth of water canals*

H *Labyrinth of water canals*

I *Garden of Silk*

K *The Rotunda Pavilion*

L *The Garden of one hundred columns.*

M *Obelisk Monument to the Sun*

Scale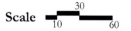

PLATE V

SCHEMATIC PLAN FOR THE PALACE & GARDENS OF QUEEN ELEUTIRILLIDE

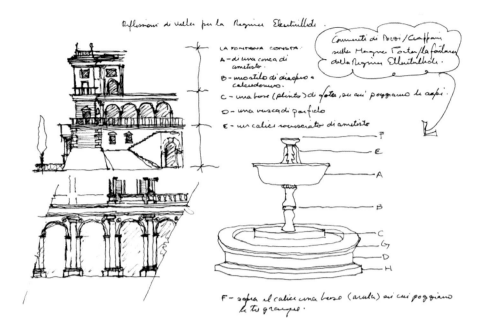

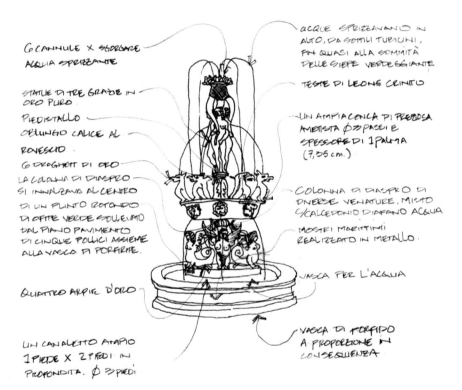

PLATE VI

SKETCHES & SCHEMATICS FOR THE PALACE & GARDENS OF

QUEEN ELEUTIRILLIDE

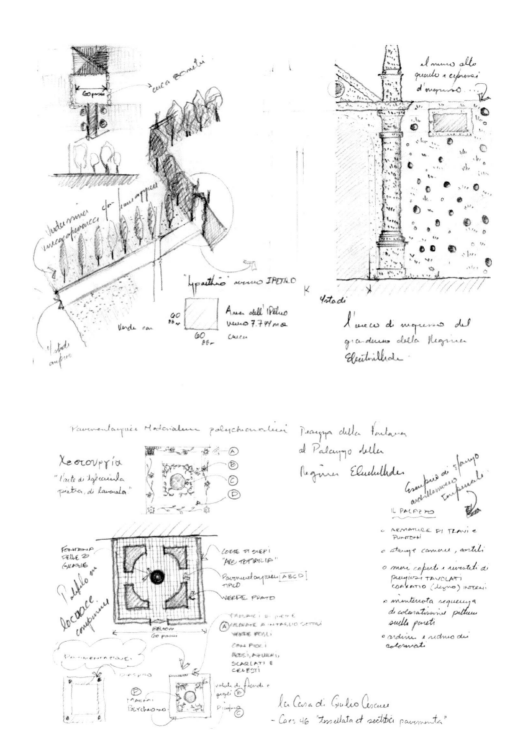

PLATE VII

SKETCHES & SCHEMATICS FOR THE PALACE & GARDENS OF

QUEEN ELEUTIRILLIDE

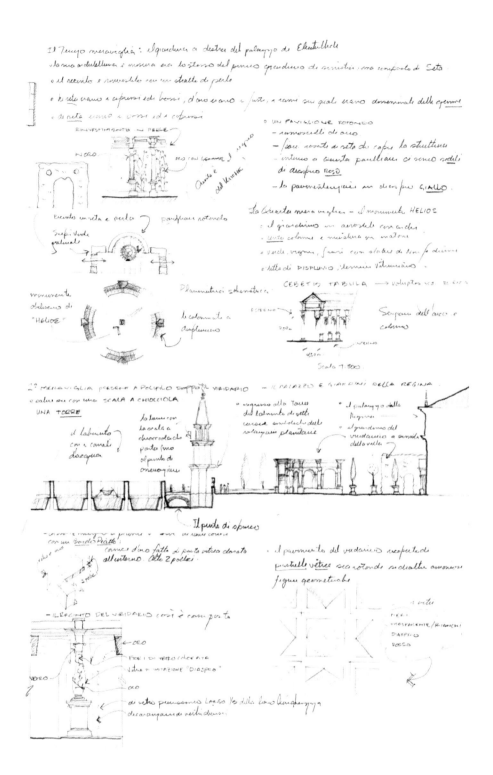

PLATE VIII

SKETCHES & SCHEMATICS FOR THE PALACE & GARDENS OF

QUEEN ELEUTIRILLIDE

CHAPTER TWO

THE GREAT PYRAMID

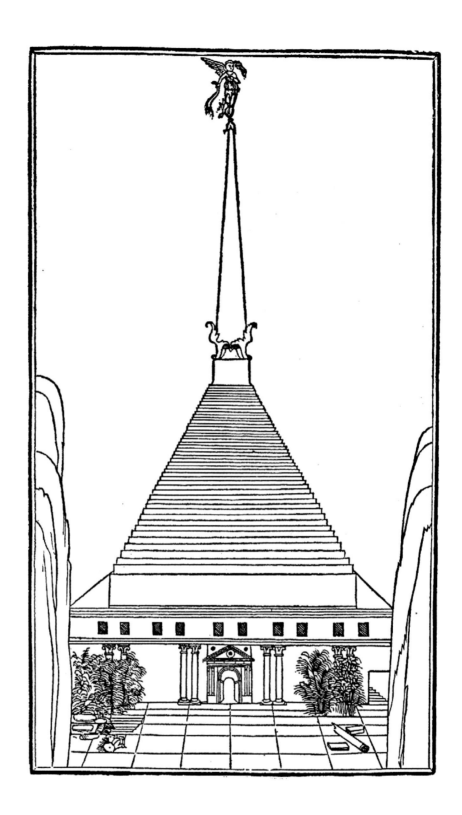

4. A Great Pyramid

"*...Cum quale temerario dunque invento di arte? Cum quale virtute & humane forcie, & ordine, & incredibile impensa cum cœlestæ æmulatione tanto nell aire tale pondo suggesto riportare?*"

"*...What bold invention of art, what power and human energy, what organization and incredible expense were needed to hoist this weight so high into the air, to rival the heavens?*"

- *Poliphilus, admiring the workmanship of the Great Pyramid* [1]

POLIPHILUS, DREAMING AGAIN AFTER A SPELL OF SLEEPLESSNESS, finds himself walking among the palm trees as if in Egypt, seemingly alone, when an open-jawed wolf appears on his left. The terrifying creature runs off inexplicably (as creatures in dreams tend to do) and Poliphilus finds himself mesmerized by an enormous building, "The more closely I approached it, the more it appeared to be a huge and magnificent object, and the greater was my desire to admire it; for now it did not look like a high watchtower, but rather a tall obelisk resting on a vast mass of stone."[2]

Poliphilus joyously examines the pyramid, composed of white square and rectangular stones placed without cement, smoothed and whose joints were treated with red clay[3], "so that the thinnest needle could not have penetrated into the borders or cracks between one edge and another."[4] He also discovered a colonnade "of the noblest form imaginable"[5] as well as roughly carved epistles and capitals, cornices, zophori and arched beams. Some elements were partly or seriously ruined: broken statues missing their brass details and other beautifully carved stone and marble reduced to unrecognizable fragments. Wild shrubs, including briars full of stinging wasps, and

5. A Great Pyramid (French Edition)

lizards took up residence among the ruins, sometimes making Poliphilus "shrink with no small horror."

Poliphilus bemoans his intellectual limitations to describe the Great Pyramid, but makes a detailed, architecturally-minded attempt, carefully measuring the dimensions of the stones and the angles at which they were placed to form a pyramid. Quite often, his disciplined description gives way to poetic awe at the beauty of the pyramid[6]:

"Above all, there was the immensity of the undertaking, the exceeding subtlety, the extravagant and acute ingenuity, the great care and exquisite diligence of the architect…What capstans and pulley blocks, what cranes, compound pulleys, frameworks of beams and other lifting machines? It is enough to silence every other structure, however large or incredible."[7]

POSITION OF THE PYRAMID:

As Poliphilus walks in a valley, encircled by pleasant hills "of no great height", he sees an incredibly tall structure and the hills surrounding the valley rising higher as they approached the Pyramid, seeming to join it. The obelisk, which seemed to block his path at the end of the valley, was higher than the surrounding summits and Poliphilus believes this would have been so even if the mountains had been as high as Mount Olympus[8]. Amid the weed-ridden, ruined walls and statues, he finds an undamaged portal, proportionate to the entire building. The stonework was continuous between the two mountains, interposed between two hanging promontories. The wings of the mountains went perpendicularly from the summit to the ground so that the structure was artificially joined to the mountains, providing protection to the valley and its inhabitants. No one could enter or exit the valley except through the portal. Above this immense construction was a "monstrous pyramid, shaped like a pointed diamond."

BASE OF THE PYRAMID

Poliphilus measures each of the four faces of the pyramid's base and finds them to be six stadia in length or a total of twenty four stadia for the equilateral base. The height of the base including the great cornice was 1/5th of a stadium.[9] If a line were raised from each corner of the base, these four lines would meet above the center to make a perfect pyramidal form. The median perpendicular above the crossing of the two diagonals of the plinth measured five/sixths of the ascending lines. Poliphilus surmises that the base of the pyramid was not built, but had been instead carved out of what had been a mountain. The rest of the steps of the pyramid were put together from separate blocks. At the front of the base, Poliphilus found a sculpture of a gigantomachy, "marvelously carved, excellently worked and lacking only the breath of life."[10] Some of the horses in the sculpture were wounded and apparently breathing their last breaths while others trampled carelessly on the fallen bodies. Some of the giants had daggers in their belts, some were dragged with their feet caught in the stirrups, some fought on foot with various weapons and shields. Poliphilus found the battle so frightening in appearance that "you would have said that bloody and valiant Mars was there fighting with Porphyrio and Alcyoneus."[11] This larger-than life image was sculptured in relief from lustrous marble, with its spaces filled by black stone. Poliphilus found the image both fascinating and tiring – so much detail that he lost track of the whole and confused the individual parts. The excessive pleasure Poliphilus finds in this and other statues reminds him of his desired Polia, his ardor for the beautiful creations so great that he momentarily stopped focusing on his "amorous and celestial ideal."

THE PYRAMID AND THE OBELISK

From the base of the pyramid to the top measured 1410 steps[12], each being a cubit high, minus ten steps where its tapering stopped "whose place was occupied by a stupendous solid and stable cube of such monstrous size that one could not believe that such a thing could even have been raised to this position."[13] The pyramid did not join the mountains flanking it but was separated by ten paces on either side. This giant monolith, created of the same Parian stone as the steps, served as the base and support for the obelisk (see fig. 6). It measured six parts along each descending side, two toward the bottom and one across its tapered top. This part rested on the upper surface of the cube, which measured four paces[14] on each side. Where the sides meet, there were "four harpy's feet of metal, with their plumage and clawed diagonals," all of proportional thickness, two paces high.[15] The obelisk rested on them, two paces wide

6. MEASUREMENTS OF THE PYRAMID'S SUMMIT WITH THE OBELISK & ITS BASE

and seven high,[16] made from mottled red Theban stone, "smooth and polished as bright as a mirror"[17] with Egyptian hieroglyphs carved on its faces.

Above this was a revolving machine or cupola, fixed on a spike. It held a statue of a nymph, with a proportion so that when an observer looked up, it had the appearance of being true-life in size.

Poliphilus was astonished, both by the height to which the statue had been raised, and by its beauty. The garments of the nymph seemed to blow in the wind as it revolved, and the placement of its wings indicated that the nymph was flying. His narration is delightful:

"ITS BEAUTIFUL FACE WAS TURNED TOWARDS THE WINGS WITH A KINDLY EXPRESSION, AND ITS TRESSES FLOATED LOOSELY ABOVE ITS FOREHEAD IN THE DIRECTION OF ITS FLIGHT, WHILE THE CROWN OR CRANIUM WAS BARE AND ALMOST HAIRLESS. IN ITS RIGHT HAND IT HELD THE OBJECT AT WHICH IT WAS LOOKING: AN ELABORATE CORNUCOPIA FILLED WITH GOOD THINGS, BUT TURNED TOWARDS THE EARTH; AND IT HELD ITS OTHER HAND TIGHTLY OVER ITS BARE BREAST. THIS STATUE REVOLVED EASILY AT EVERY BREATH OF WIND, MAKING SUCH A NOISE FROM THE FRICTION OF THE HOLLOW METAL DEVICE, AS WAS NEVER HEARD FROM THE ROMAN TREASURY. AND WHERE THE IMAGES SCRAPED AGAINST THE PEDESTAL BENEATH THEM, IT MADE A JINGLING UNMATCHED BY THE TINTINNABULUM[18] IN THE GREAT BATHS OF HADRIAN, NOR BY THAT OF THE FIVE PYRAMIDS STANDING IN A SQUARE."[19]

PASSAGEWAYS:

In the center of the plinth that lay beneath the pyramid was the serpentine head of Medusa, "howling and snarling to show its fury," with its mouth hollowed out in a straight passageway with a vaulted roof, which took a visitor to the center of the pyramid;[20] it was perfectly hollowed out, into an immense, spherical chamber one mile high, realized through a careful use of mathematical calculations on the part of the ancient architect. Poliphilus found that he could climb to the Medusa's opening "by way of the curling hair, which was formed with unimaginable cleverness and artistry." Once at the center of the pyramid, there was a winding channel with a spiral staircase, which took Poliphilus to the top of the pyramid. The spiral was brightly lit, owing to the "ingenious and gifted architect"[21] who had created a number of lighting channels that corresponded to the movements of the sun. The lower section of the pyramid was lit by the channels above it, the upper part by those below. With some reflection from the opposite walls, sufficient light filtered through to all these sections of the pyramid.

Poliphilus climbed the spiral, feeling dizzy and fatigued, but also awed by the sights. He found half-pace high metal posts, shaped like spindles, placed at 18-inch intervals around the circular opening at the top of the stairs. They were joined at the top by a curved railing, also made of metal, creating a fence around the edge of the platform. Poliphilus, who remained in the center of the platform because he was feeling off-balance, deduced the fence was created for safety reasons "to prevent anyone careless from plunging into the opening of the winding chasm."[22] Poliphilus sees a bronze plaque that includes the architect's name and the dimensions of the monument clearly indicated.[23]

Going back down towards the base of the Pyramid, Poliphilus also describes a four-sided area, or "piazza," in front of the portal that was left uncovered. He measured it at thirty paces across, paved with marble squares placed a foot apart, with interstices filled with mosaics as well as overgrowth and damaged stones. At the edges, on the left and right toward the mountains, were two orders of columns at ground level, with a space of fifteen paces between each column. Some of the columns had lost their capitals and were buried in the ruins.

In this "piazza," also near the door, there was a bronze winged horse, an elephant carrying an obelisk, and a colossus (see Chapter 3), which Poliphilus gives a fanciful account of each. His wonderment is great enough to make him momentarily forget his unrequited passion for Polia.

In his description of the Great Pyramid as with other structural marvels, Poliphilus manages to describe individual elements in minute, specific detail without losing appreciation of the overall beauty of what he sees. He switches easily from providing measurements and angles to waxing poetic about his emotional reaction. He explains that it is precisely the original architect's extreme attention to details – beginning with a square, subdivided to the smallest degree – that resulted in the faultless, breathtaking beauty of the pyramid. After describing in detail the entrance portal in the center of the base, Poliphilus was surprised by a ferocious dragon. He then fled through the portal and into the depths of the Pyramid encountering a difficult series of corridors, which he described as a labyrinth.

THE GREAT PYRAMID

LEGEND

The great obelisk & base **A**

Winding channel with a **B**
spiral stairway leading to
the pyramid's summit

Air & light channels **C**

Key stone **D**

Interior light openings **E**

Interior entrance from **F**
main portal

Hollow interior **G**

1410 steps leading to **H**
the pyramid's summit

Large plinth supporting **I**
the pyramid

Labyrinth at the base **M**
within the great hollow space

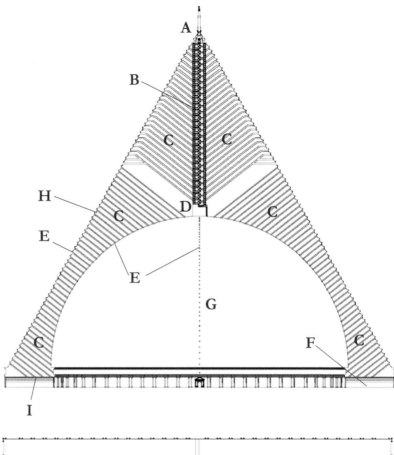

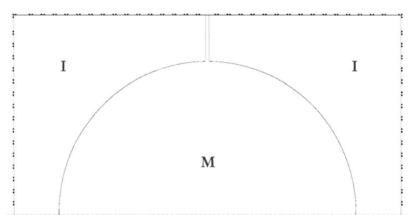

PLATE I

GENERAL PLAN & SECTION DRAWINGS
OF THE
MAIN PYRAMID COMPLEX

<u>LEGEND</u>

The great obelisk, a wind machine **A**
with the statue of Occasio (Fortune),
& supporting base in orichalcum

1410 steps **B**
leading to the pyramid's
summit (minus 10 steps)

Entrance to light channels **C**

Main portal entrace **D**

Medusa **E**

Supporting plinth with **F**
crown and aerostyle colonnade

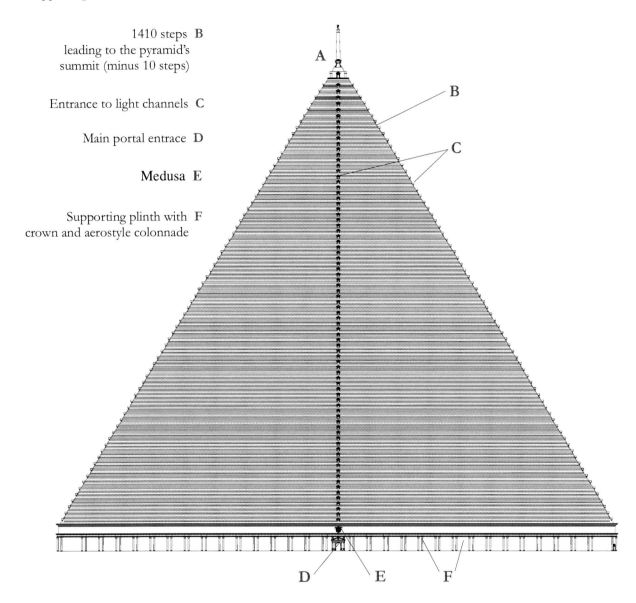

PLATE II

GENERAL FACADE
OF THE
MAIN PYRAMID COMPLEX

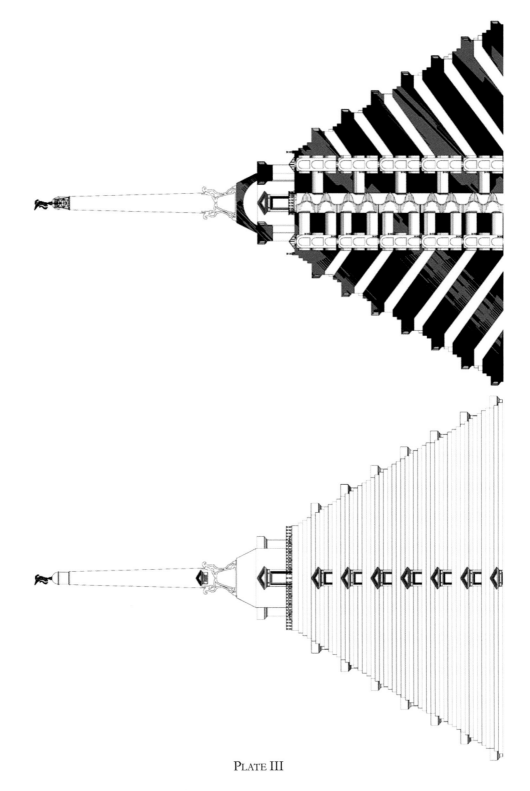

PLATE III

SECTION AND ELEVATION OF THE SUMMIT:
LIGHT CHANNELS. WINDING STAIRWAY, OBELISK, & WIND MACHINE

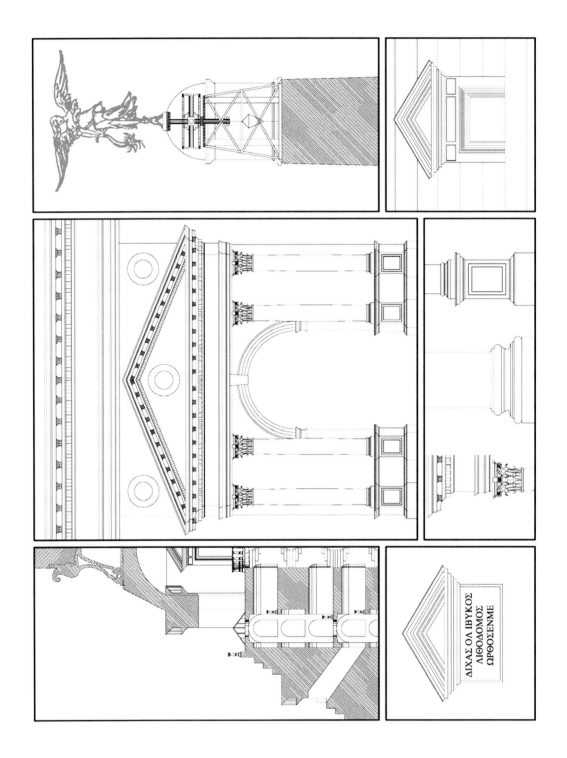

ΔΙΧΑΣ ΟΛ ΙΒΥΚΟΣ
ΛΙΘΟΔΟΜΟΣ
ΩΡΘΟΣΕΝΜΕ

PLATE IV

DRAWING DETAILS:
MAIN PORTAL, INSCRIPTIONS, WIND MACHINE,
ARCHITECTURAL ORDERS, TYPICAL LIGHT PORTAL, & SECTION OF PYRAMID SUMMIT

PLATE V

MAIN PERSPECTIVE VIEW

PLATE VI

PERSPECTIVE VIEWS OF ENTRANCE

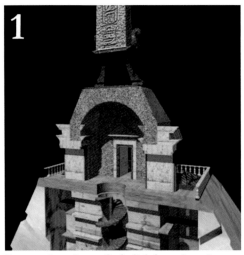

Perspective view of obelisk base interior

Perspective view of spiral stairway

Wind mechanism at the top of the obelisk

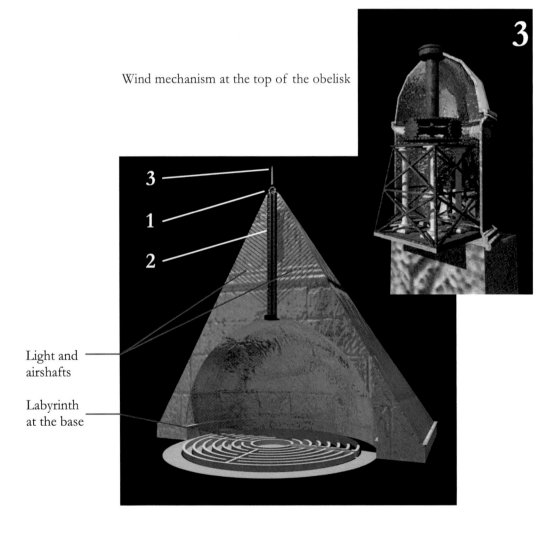

Light and airshafts

Labyrinth at the base

PLATE VII

DETAILS

PLATE VIII

EXTERIOR PERSPECTIVE VIEWS:
BASE & SUMMIT

CHAPTER THREE

THE GREAT HIPPODROMUS & ITS MONUMENTS:

A HORSE, AN ELEPHANT BEARING AN OBELISK, AND A COLOSSUS

7. An Elelphant & an Obelisk

"...Se non quandonque io applicato mirava, &
curiosamente tutte le parte al venusto composito
conveniente, examinando di quelle excellente &
eximie statue lapidee, di virginale factura, che di
subito excitato caldamente singultando
sospirava?"

"...As I marveled at it and examined carefully every part of the beautiful complex, examining these excellent and noble statues made from virgin stone, my emotions were suddenly so warmly aroused that I gave forth a sobbing sigh?"

- *Poliphilus, commenting as he takes in the sights surrounding the Great Pyramid's portal* [1]

P OLIPHILUS, BEGAN HIS DREAM WITH THE IMAGE OF HIS "DIVINE

and immeasurably desired Polia," a constant companion along his journey. But he

manages to forget about her, at least momentarily, as he rhapsodizes instead over the

magnificence of a Great Hippodromus, or square, and three statues: a horse, an

elephant and a reclining colossus.

Poliphilus laments his inability to describe the statues perfectly and bemoans the

lack of "proper vernacular and native terms peculiar to the art of architecture"[2] to

communicate his vision to readers:

"O EXECRABILE & SACRILEGA BARBARIE, COME HAI EXSPOLIABONDA IVASO, LA PIU

NOBILE PARTE DIL PRETIOSO THESORO & SACRARIO LATINO, & ARTE TANTO

DIGNIFICATA, AL PRAESENTE IFUSCATA DA MALEDICTA IGNORANTIA PERDITAMENTE

OFFENSA. LA QUALE ASSOCIATA INSEME CUM LA FREMENTE, INEXPLEBILE, & PERFIDA

AVARITIA, HA OCCAECATO QUELLA TANTO SUMMA & EXCELLENTE PARTE CHE ROMA

FECE & SUBLIME & VAGABONDA IMPERATRICE."[3]

"OH, EXECRABLE AND SACRILEGIOUS BARBARISM, HOW YOU HAVE INVADED AND SACKED THE NOBLEST PART OF THE LATIN TREASURY AND SANCTUARY! A ONCE HONORABLE ART IS NOW POLLUTED AND LOST, THANKS TO YOUR ACCURSED IGNORANCE, WHICH IS LEAGUE WITH RAGING, UNSLAKED AND PERFIDIOUS GREED HAS EXTINGUISHED THAT SUPREME AND EXCELLENT PORTION THAT MADE ROME THE SUBLIME EMPRESS OF THE WORLD."[4]

Such ravings are not uncommon, but Poliphilus can never stay angry for long: the beauty of the pyramid above soothes him, and he generously describes his vision in great detail.

8. THE UNHAPPY HORSE (EQUUS INFŒLICITATIS)

THE HORSE:

About ten paces[5] from the portal's opening towards the center of the Hippodromus, Poliphilus sees a statue of a winged horse, made of bronze. Its wings, excessively large, appear poised for flight. One of the horse's hooves covered a circle five feet in diameter, and the distance from the hooves to the horse's chest was nine feet.[6] The horse was without a bridle, and one of its ears was pointed forward and the other back. Its long mane fell over the right side of its back as a number of children attempted to ride its back. Poliphilus contends that the horse's speed and jolting make it impossible for any child to gain a seat. Some had fallen to the ground and were trying to remount, clutching the horse's leg; others were in the process of falling, but still desperately clutched the horse's mane and chest hairs, seeking purchase (fig. 8).

9. THE UNHAPPY HORSE: INSCRIPTIONS ON THE BACK & FRONT

The horse was mounted on a base. On the front of the base, the green marble was fashioned to resemble a crown of bitter parsley mixed with what were fennel leaves and an inscription in the center praising the ambiguous god (fig. 9).[7] On the opposite side of the pedestal, there was a similar crown, however with a representation of poisonous aconite leaves with a center inscription giving the name of the statuary composition in Latin letters: "the unhappy horse." [8] On the surface of the base was a plaque that also depicted the horse and children. Poliphilus marveled that the cast was made of one piece and, at the same time, considered whether the horse or its would-be jockeys had been satisfied. He decided neither were – the horse had been kept from flight by the children, and the children looked sad and weary; none appeared to have been a successful rider.

10. THE UNHAPPY HORSE: TWO-FACED FIGURES DANCING IN A CIRCLE

The base of the statue was composed of solid marble, with varicolored veins and spots mingled all over it. Sculpted to the right were figures of seven men and seven women dancing (fig. 10). Each figure had two faces, one smiling and one weeping. They danced in a circle, man-to-man, woman-to-woman, so that a sad face of one was always turned toward a happy face of the other. Beneath the dancers the word TIME was inscribed. On the other side, Poliphilus sees another work showing young people gathering flowers, plants and shrubs while nymphs playfully snatched their gathered flora away. Beneath these youthful figures was inscribed the word: LOSS.

11. THE UNHAPPY HORSE: YOUNG PEOPLE GATHERING FLOWERS

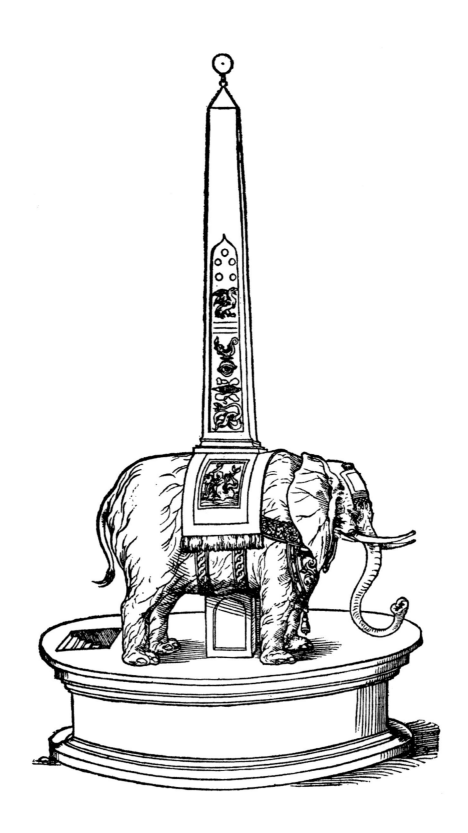

12. An Elelphant & an Obelisk (French Edition)

THE ELEPHANT, ITS BASE AND AN OBELISK:

Poliphilus also sees a statue of an elephant made of rock darker than obsidian, dusted with gold and silver. It had a saddle made of bronze, attached by stone, decorated with small figures and small scenes. The elephant's tusks were made of a bright white stone and a bronze pectoral hung beneath the saddle, which bore the following inscription: "the brain is in the head." The elephant's trunk hung in the air and its wrinkled ears hung down.

13. THE ELEPHANT'S HEADRESS

The elephant carried the burden of an elegant obelisk made from green Lacedaemonian[9] stone, decorated by Egyptian hieroglyphics on three of its faces, with the surface of the saddle having depicted "...many small figures, bosses, and little scenes and stories..."[10] The obelisk's "...width of its equal faces at the lowest point was one pace...." Poliphilus deduced that by multiplying by seven, he calculated the height of the obelisk as it tapered upwards towards its summit.[11] At this point, a round ball was stationed at its point, made from a "...shiny transparent material..."[12]

The base had Hieroglyphs "...which were carved along the oblong of the surround base, which was finished properly with the requisite *areobate*, the plinth, *gula*, torus, and *orbiculo*, its astragals...and a *cyma reversa* at the footing. The decorations above were no less proper, with the projecting *cyma reversa* and torque, *trochili*, dentils, and *astragals*...." Its composition was said to have stood firmly on a base of highly polished porphyry 12 paces long, 5 paces wide, and 3 paces high with a simple plan geometry of a rectangle with two semi-circles at its sides.[13]

Behind the elephant, Poliphilus found a small stairway carved out, with seven steps leading to a small doorway that took him to the innards of the elephant, which could be explored by climbing a ladder made of metal rungs. The elephant was empty of organs or skeletal structure except for what appeared as an inextinguishable lamp that shed enough light for him to inspect the elephant. At the back of the animal was a tomb, atop of which was a nude male, made from black stone, his teeth eyes and nails overlaid with silver. He carried a gilded scepter in his right hand and a concave shield shaped like a horse's skull in his left. Frightened by this image, Poliphilus quickly fled in the opposite direction toward the elephant's head only to encounter a similar tomb, topped by a queen. Her right hand was raised, her index finger pointing over and behind her shoulders. In her left hand was a tablet, inscribed in three languages. [14] Poliphilus found this puzzling but was too frightened to stay and try to solve its mystery. He descended the stairs and exited from the elephant, marveling, "What kind of drill or other device could have been used to pierce such hard and resistant rock and to evacuate such a mass of unyielding material, so as to make the hollow interior correspond exactly with the exterior form?"[15]

Once outside again, Poliphilus describes ancient hieroglyphics (fig. 14) chiseled along the surface of the porphyry base where he deduces on its meaning:

...Ex Labore Deo Naturae Sacrifica Liberaliter, Paulatim Reduces Animum Deo Subiectum. Firmam Custodiam Viate Tua e Misericorditer Gubernando Tenebit, Incolumem Queservabit..." [16]

14. Hieroglyphics Inscribed on the Elephant's Base

THE COLOSSUS:

Perhaps Poliphilus' trepidation regarding the elephant was precipitated by the sickly human groan he had heard when first rushing toward the giant animal. When he heard the noise, he approached it cautiously, clambering across large fragments and chips of marble until he discovered the source of the haunting noise. He was then equally nervous and excited about his finding: the moaning had been created by the wind entering the open feet of a giant, sixty paces[17] long and cast from metal. The colossus[18], a middle-aged man lying on his back, had his head propped on a pillow and appeared to be ill, making the sickly noises appropriate. Poliphilus was able to use the statue's hair, including his beard, as climbing tools and reach the open mouth. Once inside the mouth, he climbed down a set of stairs through the throat, stomach and other parts of the man's body. Illuminated tunnels provided access to all the organs, bones and muscles of the body, each of them properly named in three languages. When he reaches the heart, he is reminded again of his beloved Polia, and utters a sigh that resonated throughout the statue. He also sees near the giant the forehead of a female statue visible among the ruins, the only apparent surviving portion of the female statue. Poliphilus did not look beneath the rubble to answer this question satisfactorily as he feared injury. Before long, however, his curiosity leads him back to examine a Great Portal at the center of the plinth at the base of the Great Pyramid.

* * *

THE GREAT HIPPODROMUS:
A HORSE & AN ELEPHANT
BEARING AN OBELISK

PLATE I

PARTIAL BIRD'S EYE VIEW OF THE HIPPODROMUS "PIAZZA"
AS SEEN FROM THE SUMMIT OF THE PYRAMID *&* MAIN PERSPECTIVE VIEW
SEEN TOWARDS THE PYRAMID

TEMPVS

AMISSIO

PLATE II

THE UNHAPPY HORSE:
FACADE VIEWS OF THE BASE

PLATE III

THE UNHAPPY HORSE:
FACADE VIEWS OF THE BASE & CLOSE PERSPECTIVE VIEW

PLATE IV

THE ELEPHANT & OBELISK: PERSPECTIVE VIEW

CHAPTER FOUR

THE GRAND ARCH

15. THE GREAT ARCH

"Pervenuto dunque ad questa veterrima porta di opera molto spectabile, & cum exquisite regulatione & arte, & praeclari ornati di scalptura, & di vario liniamento maravegliosamente constructa. Per le quale tutte cose essendo io studioso & di voluptate infiammato di intendere il setoso intellecto, & la puestigatione acre dil perspicace Architecto, dilla sua dimensione, & circa il liniamento & la prattica perscrutandola subtilmente cusi io feci."

"I came, then, to this ancient portal of splendid workmanship, marvelously constructed with exquisite regularity and art, and magnificently decorated with sculpture and varied lineaments. I was inflamed with the pleasure of studying and understanding the fertile intellect and sharp intelligence of the wise architect; and thus I made this careful scrutiny of its dimensions, its lineaments, and its practical aspects."

- *Poliphilus, upon arriving at the Great Arch.* [1]

P OLIPHILUS, PROVES HIMSELF FAR MORE THAN A ROMANTIC commentator when he finds the Great Portal or Arch below the immense pyramid. He slips easily into the role of architectural professor, explaining angles, shapes and materials in language a beginning student could understand and an advanced scholar could appreciate.

MEASURING SYMMETRY:

He measures the squares beneath the columns (two on each side of the archway) and believes these four-sided figures are key to the symmetry of the portal. Each square, ABCD[2], is divided by three equidistant straight lines and three transverse lines to form sixteen squares. Add a figure half the size to the one before and twenty-four squares are created[3]. He then draws two diagonals across the first figure ABCD and then a straight and a transverse line, intersecting, to form four squares. Above the equal-sided figure, he marks four median points, joining them to create a rhombus[4].

After he recognizes this division, Poliphilus is stupefied how his contemporaries [architects] are negligent on the art of building, "…dishonoring the perfect symmetry of parts through their negligence of nature's teachings[5]…it is a golden saying and a celestial adage, that virtue and happiness reside in the mean[6]…" Such perfect symmetry should be studied by all architects, Poliphilus mandates, because in its absence, "everything will be false, because any part that does not fit with its whole is wrong."[7] . Adherence to this rule does not preclude artistry as the "clever and industrious architect can adorn his work at will with additions and subtractions so as to gratify the sight, so long as the solid body is kept intact and conciliated with the whole."[8] Poliphilus now becomes distracted by expressing the ethics of the architect, his profession, and training, as well as how works should be carried out[9]. He continues by expressing that all bodies of architecture should first be symmetrical, then adorned to be visually pleasing, but aesthetics should never come before the basics.[10]

Poliphilus continues his lesson by suggesting that the three preceding figures be reduced to a single drawing. He starts by removing the rhombus and the diagonals, the three perpendiculars and the three horizontal lines, except for the middle line that meets the perpendicular lines. This creates two perfect rectangles, each containing four squares. To determine the width of the arch and its jambs, Poliphilus draws the diagonal of the bottom rectangle and then redraws it perpendicularly toward the straight line AB. The line AB becomes the place for an extended or straight beam. The midpoint of

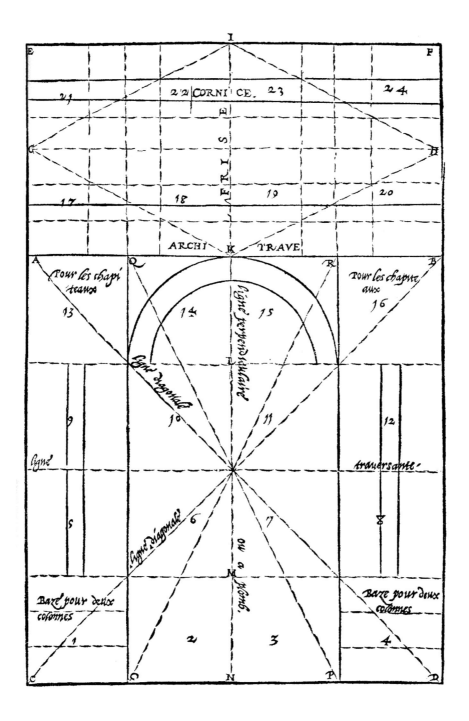

16. Proportions of the Arch (French Edition)

the truncated line EF becomes the point from which the arched beam bends in a semicircle[11]. To maintain the strength of the bent arch, Poliphilus maintains that the bend should have "as much added to its downward/pointing horns as the semidiameter of its thickness."[12]

Poliphilus continues his measuring by describing how the ancient architect arrived at the base or podium. Under the double columns on each side of the opening, he finds that the square base begins with a plinth one foot above the level of the paved area. From here, the *reversed cymas*, toruses and channels, which rose in stages toward the podium, create the bases for the anti-columns. From the top of the podium, protrudes the cornice with reversed cyma and other concurrent lineaments.

Between the line AB and the top line of the master square MN, the space is divided three times to create four parts. Three parts were assigned to the straight beam, zophurus and cornice. The corona took up a slightly disproportionate amount of space than the beam and frieze, which Poliphilus finds clever, as it permits the bottom of the sculpture beneath it to be visible. Alternately, the architect could have enlarged the ornamental part above the sculpture, but this would have disturbed the symmetry. Above this was another perfect square: the zophorus projected above the perpendicular of the columns, dividing it into two parts. There were two such squares flanking a third, which was divided into seven parts[13], the middle reserved for a niche to host a nymph's throne.

Poliphilus adds together the figure of twenty-four squares and obtains a rectangle-and-a-half, OPQT. He divides the half rectangle into six equal portions with five lines. At the midpoint of the fifth line, upwards, is the peak of the frontispiece; the lines slope down from there to cut the lateral extension of the corona. To complete his description of the ancient architect's probable proportional method, he ends by mentioning that this frontispiece corresponds with the lineaments of the dentillated cornice; its first order taken from the plane of the projecting square and its last from the cornice. Poliphilus also measured the thickness of one base and found that it was half of the lower diameter of the column. He used this finding to determine the height of the column to be more than twenty-eight cubits.

MATERIALS:

The portal was made from polished slabs of cut stone; the bases were cast from the same bronze as the capitals. The two columns next to the door were made of porphyry, which were dark red and randomly dotted with circles of a lighter color; two others were made of fluted [14], serpentine marble[15] in the Cariatic [16] fashion. To the left and the right of these columns were pairs of columns made of Laconic [17] stone. The freestanding columns made of porphyry were fluted with twenty-four channels going exactly between the fillets, the lower third of them filled with a cable. Poliphilus, after noticing the two different columns, surmises this might be because the building was ritually dedicated to both sexes (men and women or gods and goddesses) and that a greater portion was attributed to females (the fluted portion) than the male (the filled portion) "because the slippery nature of the former exceeds the latter in lasciviousness."[18] The columns rested on bases, or *stylopodium*, of bronze as were the capitals above them. Poliphilus' description is precise:

"THESE CAPITALS WERE TOPPED BY SINUOUS ABACI…DECORATED IN THE CENTER BY A LILY, WITH THEIR VASES EXCELLENTLY CLOTHED IN THE ROMAN AND CORINTHIAN

[MANNER] WITH TWO ROWS OF EIGHT ACANTHUS LEAVES. OUT OF THESE LEAVES ISSUED THE LESSER VOLUTES, TURNING TOWARD THE MIDDLE OF THE VASE AND BEARING THE LILY, WHICH WAS BEAUTIFULLY PLACED ON THE CURVE, AFTER WHICH THE STEMS CURLED DOWN BENEATH THE PROTRUSION OF THE ABACUS. AGRIPPA WAS RIGHT TO PLACE SUCH COLUMNS IN THE PRONAOS OF THE WONDERFUL PANTHEON, ADDING TO THEIR HEIGHT AN ENTIRE DIAMETER OF THE BOTTOM OF THE COLUMN AND OBSERVING THE SAME SYMMETRY IN ALL THE PARTS AND ACCESSORIES."[19]

The threshold of the doorway was made from leek-green stone that was marred by a scattering of black and grey spots as well as other stains. The capitals were made of the same stone, while the statues were set up against a background of coral stone, giving the figures a pink, flesh-like lighting. Other materials included a dense black stone from which an eagle was carved, a white vein of agate or onyx from which a delicate boy was crafted and another bird from sard.[20]

Only after Poliphilus details the measurements of the portal does he permit himself the luxury of extolling its beautiful ornamentation. As he says, "to the serious architect, being comes before well-being." Just as a musician divides a scale into small notes, an architect must divide a building into squares, "which is subdivided to the smallest degree to give the building its harmony and consistency and to make the parts correlate with the whole."[21]

17. THE GREAT ARCH (FRENCH EDITION)

SCULPTURES AND CARVINGS:

Against a background of coral-colored stone, Poliphilus finds a sculpted image of a bearded older man sitting on a sculpted rock and wearing a goatskin knotted above his hips. In front was an anvil fixed in a tree trunk, which served as a bench for the man's creation – a pair of glowing wings. Beside the man stood a winged lady holding onto a naked infant son, which was so delicately featured that Poliphilus (feeling poetic again) was certain she was loved by all the other statues. The potential suitors included an angry armed man and a youth, visible only from the waist up and dressed in thin material. On the left pedestal, Poliphilus sees a nude, virile man wearing partially laced boots, protruding from which were a wing on each of his feet. The same winged lady appears here, offering her child to the man (now winged himself) for a bow-and-arrow lesson. The armed man is also here, joined by a helmeted woman who held a trophy made from ancient cuirass on a spear. Atop this was a sphere with two wings, inscribed below: "Nihil firmum."[22]

Also in the doorway was an eagle, sculpted almost freestanding of black stone, its wings spread and its talons clutching a young boy by his garments. The child, hanging and naked from the waist down, appeared to be afraid of falling. Perhaps the child should have been more fearful of the eagle's "libidinous intentions"[23] characterized by a playful tongue and upright feathers.

In the triangles made by the arch was a sculpted cameo of a Victory, a barefooted, bare breasted virgin, holding onto a trophy of victory. The triangular area was filled with black stone, a sharp contrast to the milky white nymphs. Above rested the zophorus, from which was hanging a hooked tablet of metal and a Greek epigram in elegant capital letters inlayed with refined silver, to the Goddess Venus and her son:

"ΘΟΙΣ ΑΦΡΟΔΙΤΗΙ ΚΑΙ ΤΩΙ ΥΙΩΙ ΕΡΩΤΙ ΔΙΟΝΥΣΟΣ ΚΑΙ ΔΗΜΗΤΡΑ ΕΚΤΟΝ ΙΔΙΩΝ ΜΗΤΡΙ ΣΥΜΠΑΘΕΣΤΑΤΗΙ"[24]. On the front of the zophorus were trophies and weapons.

The cornice followed and above this was a bas-relief of a nymph, holding an extinguished torch toward the ground and a lighted one up to the sun.

Poliphilus sees in a square to the right the goddess Clymene, daughter of the ocean Titan and mother to Atlas, depicted here weeping after being spurned by Phoebus, the Radiant One.[25] In a square to the left, the drama continues with a depiction of Cyparissus, one of Apollo's lovers who becomes disconsolate after accidentally killing a deer that Apollo had given him. Apollo weeps also, bitterly. On a third square is a sculpture of Leucothea,[26] who was slain by her own father, and on the fourth is Daphne,[27] about to lose her virginity to Delos, when she turns into a laurel tree.

On the frontispiece, Poliphilus finds a wreath of green stone, held by two beings, which were part women, part-fish. These semi-sea creatures appear to Poliphilus to be maidens, with their hair twisted and arranged around their heads, some falling down in ringlets, and with wings jutting out of their shoulders and curling toward their tails. The wreath is inhabited by a mother goat nursing a child who grabs onto the goat's hair. A nymph inside the wreath holds onto one of the goat's feet in one hand and directs the animal's teat to the child. Another nymph encircles the goat's neck with one arm and restrains it by the horns with another. A third nymph is standing in the center, holding a branch in one hand and a drinking cup in another. Two others leap-dance between the first three.

On the flat surface beneath the order of the topmost cornice, there appeared two words in perfect [Greek] capital letters: "ΔΙΟΣ ΑΙΓΙΟΧΙΟ"[28]

Poliphilus marvels again at the symmetry and how they seem to follow the rules of the human body – as a man needs large feet beneath robust legs to support him, so does a building need stout piers at its base and, then, for aesthetic pleasure, Corinthian and Ionic columns. The parts of the portal had both harmony and beauty. Marble was used both for its strength and its allure and colors were carefully chosen: porphyry, serpentine, Numidian[29] marble, alabaster, marble with fiery spots, Spartan[30] marble, white marble, veined marble of assorted hues. The splendor of the architecture makes Poliphilus suppose that the creator had been using soft chalk or clay rather than hard stone and he finds himself hungering to view it again and again, pining almost as woefully for the ancient art as for his beloved Polia.

Feeling too deprived of the portal's wonder to move onward, Poliphilus opts to return inside the archway to rediscover the structure and ornamentation. Even the ruined fragments cause him to gaze insatiably and he delights in both reviewing sights already seen and others missed during earlier viewing. He finds on the ceiling, for instance, carvings of semi-human sea monsters embraced by women with fish-like tails sitting on their backs. Some of the women were seated in dolphin-drawn chariots, some played instruments, some were crowned with water lilies and some had fruit-filled vases. Some of the women fought each other, but the general atmosphere was game-like and lascivious. On the voussoirs of the portal, he saw several scenes depicted on a frieze: Europa swimming to Crete[31] upon a seductive bull, and her father commanding Europa's brothers to rescue her; the brother's consultation with the oracle who tells them to stop fighting dragons and to build a city where their cow lay mooing instead and other pictures in the mosaic that completed the fable – the building of Athens in Boeotia,[32] Phoenicia and Cilicia.

LOST IN A DRAGON'S LAIR:

Poliphilus also admires the "lewd Pasiphae inflamed with infamous passion: as she tries to hide herself from a robust bull, the Minotaur imprisoned in a labyrinth. The scene continues while Daedalus makes wings for himself and his son to trying to escape, but the son drowns because he failed to obey his father's orders. And, in the final scene, Daedalus hanging up the oar-like device, he made an offering to the gods.[33] Lost in the stories and in the artistry of the works that tell the tales, Poliphilus pays little attention to where he is going and finds himself at the end of a dark hallway. He begins to turn around and retrace his steps when he hears a "sound like the dragging of a great bull's carcass over the rough and ruin-strewn ground."[34] And then the deafening hiss of a giant serpent sends him running back toward the dark hallway. He runs through a maze, often forced to retrace his steps, his arms outstretched to avoid running into pillars as he flees. He believes himself in mortal danger, comparing his plight to those of the Greek gods and goddesses – Mercury when he was turned into an ibis, Diana when she was made a cholomene bird, Pan into a double form, Apollo exiled in Thrace and so on.[35] Bats fly above his head in the darkness, making Poliphilus fear that he is in the dragon's grip.[36] He contemplates death, believing it would be preferable to a dragon encounter, but the still unconsummated love of Polia spurs him on. Flooded with fear and poetic anguish, Poliphilus loses strength but, before hope vanishes, a tiny light appears. Poliphilus uses his reserve of energy to hasten toward it and finds himself in a beautiful country filled with merry maidens who lead him to the gardens of Queen Eleutirillide.

PLATES

THE GRAND ARCH

PLATE I

MAIN PERSPECTIVE VIEW

PLATE II

TOP PERSPECTIVE VIEW

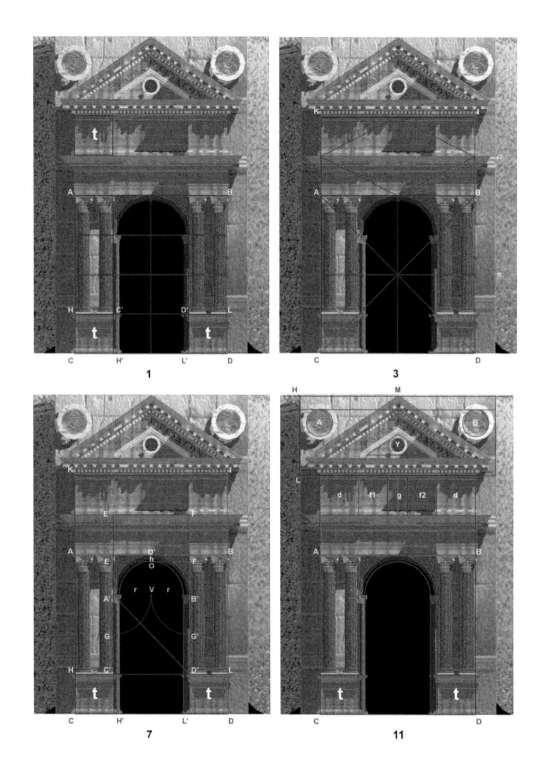

PLATE III

PROPORTIONS

CHAPTER FIVE

PALACE AND GARDENS OF
QUEEN ELEUTIRILLIDE (LIBERTY)

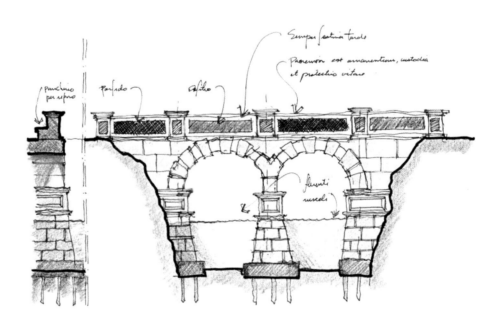

18. Poliphilus Flees a Dragon at the Portal's Entrance

19. Concept Sketch of the Marble Bridge

"…Quale marmori, quale sculpture, Ove mirai le virtute Herculane in petra luculea Semidiuvulse mirabilmente excalpte. Exuvie, statue, Tituli, & Tropæi, mirisicamente cœlati… Ad questo debitamente ceda Tito Cæsare cum le sue petre phœnicie speculabile & terse, tale & tanto che exile qualunque fœtoso ingegno se damnarebbe volendolo narrare… Perdase quivi qualunque altro mirando ædificamento…"

"… What marbles, what sculptures I saw there! There were the Labours of Hercules marvellously sculpted in high relief from translucent stone, beside spoils, statues, inscriptions and trophies miraculously carved…The Emperor Titus, with his Phoenician marble polished like a mirror, would have to give way to this. It was such that the most gifted narrator would come to grief in trying to describe it…Any other wondrous building was lost beside it…"

- *Poliphilus, when he first encounters the palace of Queen Eleutirillide.* [1]

POLIPHILUS, DRAGON'S BREATH METAPHORICALLY SINGEING HIS heels, finds outside the Great Portal a fragrant, flowering woodland at the base of a mountain. Amid the damp grass, which cools Poliphilus' body and spirit, is a high-arched marble bridge[2] that spans two running brooks. He slows to examine rectangular panels with Egyptian hieroglyphs, which he finds in the middle of each of the structure's parapets. To the right of his path, is a panel that includes carvings of an antique helmet crested with a dog's head, an ox skull with branches tied to its horns, an ancient lamp and the inscription: "Patience is the Ornament, Guardian and Protector of Life."[3] To his left he sees a carving of a circle and a dolphin entwined around an anchor and the message: Always hasten slowly[4].

20. Festina Lente

Frightened, Poliphilus doesn't precisely heed the advice. It took more than a little while for him to be reassured that the five nymphs were not to be as equally feared as the dragon he had just escaped. Stunned by their beauty and grace, Poliphilus thought he had left the earthly plane for another, more celestial realm and fretted that he had invaded a sacred place. The nymphs, curious about the quaking stranger, observed Poliphilus in silence, and then promised him safety, and freedom from even slight unpleasantness. All they asked is that Poliphilus introduce himself, which, after prostrating himself at their virginal feet, he did:

"Blessed nymphs," said Poliphilus, "I am the most ill-favoured and unhappy lover that the world has ever seen. I love – but where is she whom I love so ardently and desire with all my heart? I know not, not even where I am myself. I have arrived here after passing through more moral peril than I could ever describe." [5]

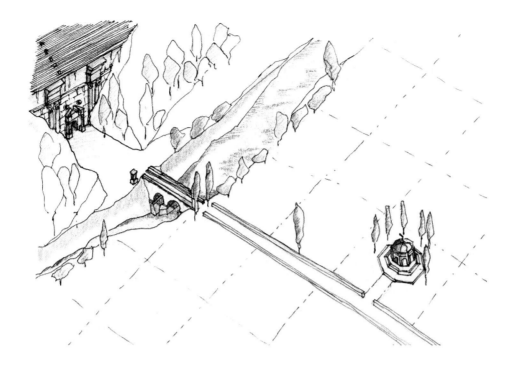

21. CONCEPTUAL SKETCH RELATING TO POLIPHILUS '

PASSAGE: FROM OBSCURITY TO THE BATH.

The sympathetic maidens lift Poliphilus onto his feet and tell him that he has entered a region of pleasure and delight and that they will be his guides to its many joys as well as introduce him to their magnificent and generous Queen Eleutirillide.[6] Giggling and laughing, the nymphs lead Poliphilus to the baths. They coax the timid mortal into the warm springs, where he dances happily while longing still for his absent love, Polia. He describes the voluptuous and lascivious movements of the nymphs in great detail while also giving careful attention to the octagonal bath building in which they frolicked.

THE BATH EXTERIOR:

The marble façade of this building had a pair of pilasters at every external angle, joined by aereobates[7] at ground level. The pilasters protruded from the solid wall by a third of their width, while their capitals, supporting the straight beam with a frieze, below

22. THE BATH: EXTERIOR & INTERIOR VIEWS (FRENCH EDITION)

a continuous cornice. The frieze had decorations with sculptures, including those of naked *putti* whose hands held nooses of woven twigs and leaves tied together by ribbons. A lead roofed octagonal dome rose above the cornice[8], perforated between the angles by panes of pure crystal. The parts of the internal vault that were not filled with crystal were coloured with Armenian blue and studded with gilded bosses.

The pinnacle rested on a high spire that followed the octagonal form of the cupola, which was topped by a sphere. Atop this point, there was a fixed stylus that fitted into another, but this one mobile, which freely revolved on itself. When the wind came, the hollow spire rotated, together with a ball at its summit that was a third of the size of the lower ball. On top of the ball stood a naked child on one leg, his left hanging freely. The back of the child's head was hollow, pierced through as far as his mouth, to which a trumpet was attached. Between the two balls was a wing, which impelled the higher ball and the child. When the back of the child faced the wind, the trumpet sounded as if he had actually blown into it himself.

The Bath Interior:

Inside the bath building were four rows of seats made from continuously jointed jasper and chalcedony[9] stone slabs of every colour. The lower two seats were covered with warm water, which aligned with the surface of the third. In each angle there was a detached Corinthian column composed of jasper whose undulating veins were evident. The columns supported the capitals beneath a beam above, which lay the zophori, which was decorated with putti playing in the water with aquatic beasts. This was capped by a cornice; above the projection of the colonettes there was a garland of oak leaves, composed of green jasper and tied with gilded ribbons.

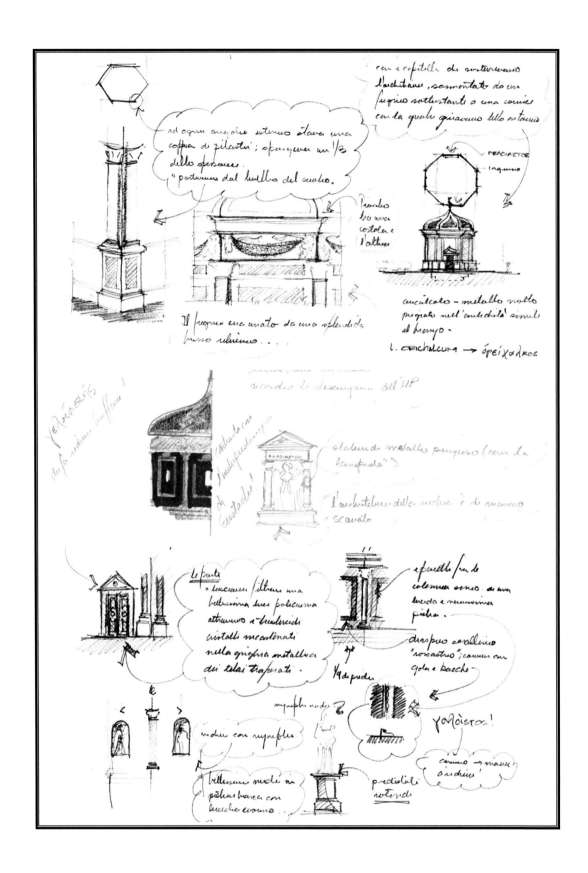

23. The Bath: Architectural Conceptual Sketches

A shaggy-maned lion that held a ring in its teeth filled the convex of the bath's domed roof.

The nymphs filled a vase with "fiery material"[10] that spewed from a fissure in the ground and placed on it fragrant gums and woods. Poliphilus inhaled the steamy perfume with delight while also amusing himself by comparing the animated nymphs cavorting with him in the baths to the nymphs carved of ivory and placed on pedestals between the columns. The paved floor beneath the pure, clear water was inlaid with stone emblems, and on the seats of the bath were inlayed mosaic fish, which appeared to be real and swimming. Above the entrance door, Poliphilus saw a dolphin of milk stone in a niche; sitting on top of the animal was a boy playing a lyre. On the opposite side of the "Geloiastos" fountain (described in the next paragraph), a swimming dolphin had been sculpted.

The fun-loving nymphs played several tricks on the innocent Poliphilus, whose senses were raw from the exquisite beauty of the bath and its virginal inhabitants as well as his constant longing for his beloved Polia. The first trick was a seemingly innocuous request by a nymph named Achoe,[11] in which Poliphilus was to fill a crystal base with cool water. Eager to please, Poliphilus started across the bath only to be hit in the face with freezing water that squirted through the penis of a statuary boy held aloft by stone nymphs along one of the interior walls of the bath. The force of the frigid water made Poliphilus fall down, much to the laughing merriment of the five nymphs.[12] When Poliphilus recovered his balance, he discovered the architect's contraption: the bottom step near the fountain was sensitive to pressure. Any weight would depress the step and raise "little Priapus'" instrument.

24. ELEUTIRILLIDE'S FOUNTAIN

Soon the nymphs and Poliphilus exited the water, dried and dressed themselves. They ate, drank and anointed themselves with fragrant creams. This was the second trick the nymphs played on Poliphilus. One of the creams they offered created in Poliphilus a sexual arousal and lust he had never before experienced. The giggling nymphs led Poliphilus on an exhausting chase through the woods, stopping only when they were certain that his passion had been trumped by fatigue.[13]

THE PALACE COURTYARD AND FOUNTAIN:

They came to a road four stadia long[14] lined with tall cypress trees, leading towards a hedged enclosure, whose entrance was as wide as the spaces between the cypresses. The enclosure or courtyard, Poliphilus noticed, was equilateral and composed of three sides resembling perpendicular walls as high as the tall cypresses along the road. All were made from citrons, oranges and lemons, about six feet[15] thick. There was an archway in the middle, shaped from the same trees, and a window above. Once inside, Poliphilus noticed that this cloister was in front of a palace, symmetrical in its architecture, which made a fourth wing for the green enclosure. It was sixty paces wide[16], and this was the dimension of the square open-air courtyard.[17]

In the centre of the courtyard, Poliphilus saw a fountain that sent clear water through narrow pipes as high as the enclosing green enclosure. The water fell back into a wide shell of amethyst[18]; three paces in diameter and three inches thick, finishing up to one inch at the rim of the tub. Aquatic monsters in bas-relief were visible all around. The fountain was fixed on a pillar of jasper, inlaid with chalcedony, which had the colour of seawater. It was made from two bases, placed atop each other, separated by a tight knot. This was then fastened to the centre of a circular plinth of greenish serpentine[19].

The plinth was raised five inches[20] above the flooring in the same manner as its rim made from porphyry. Beneath the basin and around the pillar, four golden harpies with ferocious taloned feet rested on the serpentine plinth. Their backs were shown against the central pillar, and their unfolded wings rose toward the porphyry rim of the basin. Their guises were virginal, while their hair flowed down their necks on to their shoulders, not allowing their heads to reach the underside of the basin. Their green, serpentine tails curled up, while covered with antique rinceaux[21] towards the end, joining the flower vase of the pillar. Inside the amethyst basin, there was a vase that looked like a long inverted calyx[22], which was higher than the surrounding rim as the basin was deep. Atop this was a basic support for three nude gold Graces, connected to each other. Thin streams of water flowed from their nipples. Each held in her right hand a cornucopia that reached slightly above her head allowing the mouths of all three horns to meet, making a single round opening. The cornucopia horns were decorated extravagantly with an abundance of many fruits and leaves, which overflowed from their openings.

Six spouts were protruded from the fruits and foliage, while the water flowed through them. Each of the Graces used her left hand to cover her private parts; such modesty, Poliphilus noted, also kept their elbows from colliding. The open basin's circumference reached a foot[23] beyond that of the serpentine plinth below it. Around its rim were six dragons, resting on reptilian feet with their heads pointed upward. The water coming from the Graces' breasts fell directly into the hollow and open heads of the dragons, which then spewed from the dragons' open mouths. This water then fell between the round serpentine plinth and the circle of porphyry, which rose an equal distance above the floor of the courtyard. A channel, one-and-a-half feet wide and two feet deep,[24] ran between the serpentine plinth and the porphyry circle, which was three feet[25] wide on its flat surface.

Poliphilus continues by noticing that the dragons slithered across the shallow basin with their tails coming together transforming into antique rinceaux, "making at the appropriate height a satisfying juncture"[26] with the structural support of the three figures, while at the same time not deforming "the hollow of the precious basin"[27] below. The basin was beautifully coloured by combining a green orange tree hedge, with the translucent amethyst of its composition, along with pure water "so that is resembled a rainbow among the clouds."[28] The fountain also included lion heads with manes; these stood out from the convex part of the basin, and were equally spaced between each pair of the scaly dragons. The water that fell from the six pipes of the cornucopia was spewed from the lions' mouth, falling between the dragons into the basin. Driven by low pressure, the water made a tinkling noise when it reached the basin.

The area surrounding the fountain was paved with squares of various-coloured marble and inlaid with rounds of decorative jasper,[29] somewhat smaller in diameter, and contrasting in colour to the squares. The remaining angles were filled with curling fronds and lilies. Between the squares were wide stripes, mosaic work from tiny stones depicting green leaves with blue, purple, red and yellow flowers. Poliphilus wanted to linger, to revel longer in the splendour of the fountain, but he was forced to keep pace with his talkative, swift-moving guides.

"It was," Poliphilus marvelled, "a rare work, this proud fountain erected with keen ingenuity, with its perfect harpies and the rare dignity of the support for the three brilliant golden figures, all executed with the highest artistry and finish. I could never make a brief and lucid exposition of it, much less describe it all. It was no work of merely human skills but I can freely testify, calling the gods to witness, that never in our age has there been a more graceful of admirable sculpture, nor even one to equal it."[30]

25. ELEUTIRILLIDE'S THRONE ROOM

THE PALACE FAÇADE COURTYARD:

Poliphilus could no long mourn the passing of the fountain, however, as he was seen enraptured with the palace that lay just beyond it. His eyes feasted on a cornucopia of architectural delights, including a podium, propylaeum and two hundred columns composed of Claudian, Carystean, Synnadic, and Numidian stones, all equally distributed.[31] A multi-coloured curtain woven from gold thread depicting two figures, blocked the portal entrance to this magnificent palace: one figure was surrounded by tools and the other represented was represented lifting her virginal face to the sky. The nymphs explained to Poliphilus that a vigilant maiden named Cinosia would open the curtain, which then happened shortly right after. Another curtain, dyed in every colour and embroidered with assorted shapes, plants and animals, lay ahead of the first and was drawn by a woman named Indalomena. The third and final curtain, embroidered with speeches and sayings, was opened by a woman named Mnemosyna, who advised Poliphilus that all would be well if he obeyed the Queen's kind counsel.[32]

Poliphilus' eyes were immediately struck by a "stupendous and spacious" court that joined to the side of the palace opposite the first one and was perfectly square.[33] The pavement, set inside mosaic, was made from sixty-four squares, each three feet across[34]. The squares were arranged like a chess board, alternately of coloured jasper and of bright green with sanguine spots, closely fitted that the joints were not visible. This was surrounded by a pace-wide frieze, made from stone mosaic and assembled in tiny shapes made from precious stones. Again, no joints were visible, and the stone was polished like a mirror "and made so evenly with rule and square that a spherical object placed there would never be at rest." [35]

Beyond this floor pattern, Poliphilus mentioned that there was a three-paced wide design of jaspers, prases, chalcedonies, agates and other precious stones. Seats set against the wall of this area were made of red and yellow sandalwood, dressed with green velvet and filled with wool. Poliphilus admired the walls of the enclosure, covered with plates of engraved gold. He mentions that the smooth flat surface of the plaques was divided by small pilasters into a number of rectangles with a circular wreath applied to the centre of each. It resembled fringed leaves that closely overlapped, adorned by winding ribbons. Fruits of assorted gems could be seen here and there among the leaves. In the remaining spaces between the wreaths, Poliphilus saw the seven planets depicted with priceless gems. The left hand wall was similarly divided and adorned with similar wreaths. On this wall were depicted the seven triumphs of the subjects ruled by the planets. On the right hand wall, the seven harmonies of the planets and the transit of the soul receiving the qualities of the seven degrees were depicted.

The fourth wall along the façade of the Palace, was arranged like the other three, except that the middle space was occupied by the door. The rest of the wall looked much like the others; on this the operation of the planetary virtues were depicted within the wreaths. The wreath containing the seventh planet, Sol, was above the door, higher than the others, because this is where the Queen's throne was situated. Each wall of the courtyard was twenty-eight paces[36] long, and each corresponded to the other down to the smallest details. Visitors to the open-air courtyard could find shade beneath canopies of gold beams positioned above.

Poliphilus continues by mentioning that the pilasters or semi-square columns were set four paces apart, which created seven equal divisions and were composed of lapis-lazuli[37] and tiny gold sparkles. The front of the pilasters between the enclosures was of equal height and width and carved with greenery, monsters, cornucopia, leaf-covered heads, and candelabra. All were carved in relief as detached from their background. Above the capitals were spiral-carved beams and above those the zophori[38], which included an alternating pattern of ribbon-tied greenery and dolphins. The zophori were crowned with a cornice, which above this, were positioned three-foot high vases, placed in regular intervals, and made from chalcedony, agate, amethyst, garnet and jasper.

Above these were seven-foot squared beams of bright gold. Similar beams were joined horizontally above these, creating a base for a topiary arrangement that included vines of gold, and gemstones shaped like fruit. Poliphilus wondered how it had been accomplished:

"What art, what bold ambition, what steadfast will had assembled them so perfectly? Was it done with sculptor's adhesive, or soldering, or hammering, or with the founder's art? It seemed to me impossible that a roof so wide and with such excellent joints should have been made by any of these three methods of metal-working." [39]

QUEEN ELEUTIRILLIDE:

At first, the queen listens to the nymphs and then to Poliphilus as he recounts his journey to the palace and his escape from the dragon and the dark caves. She then kindly invites him to dine with the nymphs, noble ladies and Her Majesty. Though reassured by the queen, Poliphilus remains timid as well as ashamed of his appearance – his toga is covered with burs – but his keen eye continues to take careful note of his surroundings and he enjoys the attention of the servants (with all their sensual qualities), who artfully serve a seven-course meal and occasionally wipe his face clean with silk napkins, never using the same napkin twice.

Poliphilus sees a portal made of jasper opposite the Queen's throne. First the queen, and then the reclining guests washed their hands in a portable fountain that emptied into a golden basin which recycled the water by itself; it was on wheels so that it movable along the table. The centre of the fountain was studded with round gems and topped by two vases; the top was formed into a flower with a pear-shaped diamond on top. The fountain was filled with water scented by roses, sugar, lemon peel and amber.

Our narrator tells us that the air was also perfumed by bowls set atop a gold vase and filled with boiling water, some scented with rose, others with orange, myrtle, laurel and elderflowers. Its base was set on harpy's feet and joined by foliage to a triangular support. Three naked boys stood above this, each two cubits high and standing closely together, while their winged shoulders were adjacent to each other. They rested with their right feet on a corner of the base while their left feet were relaxed and free. Each held both elbows raised, holding in each hand a baluster, which opened into a broad and shallow bowl with a wide rim. There were six of these in the circle. In the centre of the base, behind the backsides of the boys, was a column that held another bowl to be filled with scented water.

Poliphilus finds himself on sensory overdrive amid the majestic architecture, the extravagant seven-course meal and the three ballets performed afterward. Finally, the queen sends him on his way, telling him to pursue "the amorous flames of Polia" by travelling to three portals and carefully choosing which one to enter[40]. She assures him a safe trip by offering two of her handmaidens to accompany him. The queen also gives Poliphilus a gold ring set with an ananchitis[41] stone. She tells him that the handmaidens will help him choose the correct portal and will present him to another queen, who might be helpful or its opposite. The two women, Logistica and Thelemia, take Poliphilus by the hand and lead him back the hedge of orange trees from where they had first entered the palace grounds. They tell him, however, that there are several more sights for him to behold before exiting and continuing on his journey.

THE GLASS GARDEN[42]

They walked to an orchard on the left side of the palace. Poliphilus noticed that there were flowerbeds that contained plants of clear glass, topiary box trees moulded of glass and golden stems. The boxes were one pace high and the stems inside two paces tall. The beds were filled with imitation flowers and adorned with glass plaques gilded on the inside and framed in gold. The plaques continued around the beds, the lower socle two inches high. The orchard was fenced by swelling columns of glass and gold; on either side of the columns were protrusions of gold fluted pilasters, arching over from one to another. The body of the columns was an imitation of jasper and vines protruded from the solid surface. The vaults of the arches were filled with glass lozenges, a third as long as they were wide, also enclosed in framed and surrounded by encaustic paintings. The orchard was paved with small glass roundels and "appropriate and supremely graceful figures"[43] and the flowers, rubbed with an ointment and watered down, were quite fragrant.[44]

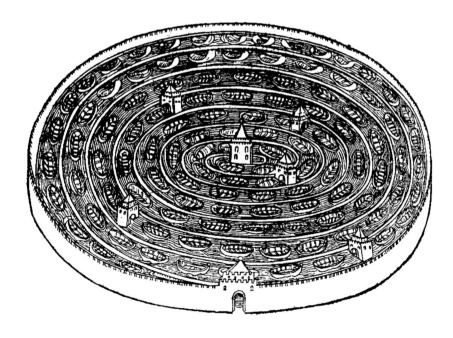

26. THE WATER LABYRINTH (FRENCH EDITION)

THE AQUATIC LABYRINTH AND THE SEVEN TOWERS

The second site remaining was to be seen from a tower[45] adjacent to the glass garden, reached by climbing a spiral staircase. From atop, Poliphilus and his companions were able to see a wide and circular garden, which was composed of a complex labyrinth; in place of streets were rivulets of water. Logistica warns Poliphilus that once the garden is entered, there is no turning back. Seven internal towers divide seven circuits of the garden[46]. A ferocious dragon dwells in the open entrance of the central tower but does not remain there; he moves from one to another. If anyone tried to enter a tower blocked by a dragon, that person would be killed.[47]

The first tower[48] is entered easily by boat; travellers enjoy a light wind to their backs, while fruits and flowers fall gently into their vessel as they make their way to the second tower. The air at the first tower is quite clear and will remain so until the middle tower is reached; then the air will darken gradually; the last tower will be lightless. In the first tower, a pious matron stands before an urn containing fates. She gives a fate to each person who enters before navigating the first circuit.

At the second tower, girls greet the travellers and ask them for their fates, aligning themselves as guides according to a person's destiny. This girl will guide the visitor to the third tower unless he decides to join another along the way.

When visitors leave the second tower for the third, they will find the water rough and will need oars to navigate. The water will become even more contrary between the third and fourth towers, although the trip will not be without pleasure. At the fourth tower, travellers are greeted by "maidens who are athletic and aggressive"[49] and who will accompany only those whose fates they find suitable. The other travellers will be forced to continue with the girls they came with, putting them at a disadvantage, as the water here becomes very difficult and requires great effort in rowing.

At the fifth tower, the water becomes very smooth, and travellers entertain themselves by admiring their images, which does not prepare them for the difficult task of passing through this tower. Logistica tells Poliphilus that one of the golden sayings, "Blessed are they who keep to the mean" [50] is illustrated at this tower. It is not a linear mean but a midpoint between what is the path and the end. "A sincere examination reveals this mean, at which one gathers the happiness or blessings either of intelligence or of riches; but if one does not have them, it is more difficult to acquire them in what follows." [51]

As they travel away from the fifth tower and toward the sixth, the water grows calmer, with little effort needed in rowing. At the sixth tower, travellers find elegant ladies with chaste and modest impressions. The visitors abandon their athletic companions for these more tranquil, religious women, who calmly "traverse the seven revolutions." [52]

Once our protagonists undergo this part, the air grows misty while the water turns rapid, and the travellers must endure a whirlpool to get to the central tower. As Logistica tells Poliphilus, "With great affliction of soul, one recalls the beautiful places and the company left behind, and is all the more aware of being unable to reverse the prow of one's boat, because the prows of the other boats are continually at one's stern."[53] By this point in the journey, travellers regret entering the labyrinth, despite its many pleasures, because it leads them to a miserable end.

At the entrance of this last tower sits a judge who holds a scale and passes judgement on those who enter. Depending on the balance, she gives them either a better or worse fate than they had upon entry.

27. THE GARDEN OF SILK WITH A RUSTIC HUT (FRENCH EDITION)

THE GARDEN OF SILK

To the right of the Queen's palace is a garden of the same size and with similar architectural arrangements as the glass garden. The construction of the dividing walls, though, was made from silk. There were silken box trees and cypresses with golden stems and branches, respectively seeded with gems. The surrounding enclosures were made from pearl. All of the surfaces were covered with clear, medium-sized pearls, while extensive green ivy grew over them, its leaves hanging down in front of the pearls.

The golden stems were bent into serpentine shapes, the tendrils creeping around the pearls with gemstone berries attached to pearl clusters. Square pilasters with golden capitals and a sequence of beams, zophori and gold coronas divided the enclosure.

28. THE DISPLUVIUM & THE MONUMENT TO THE DIVINE TRINITY (FRENCH EDITION)

The façades of the containers were inlaid with gold, silver and silken threads depicting scenes of love and hunting. It seemed to Poliphilus that the ground surface was composed of green silken velvet. In the centre of this was a round enclosure with a tall cupola composed of golden rods and covered with golden, flower rosebushes. Beneath the roof was a circle of seats made from reddish jasper, with its inside being composed of a solid circle of yellow jasper.

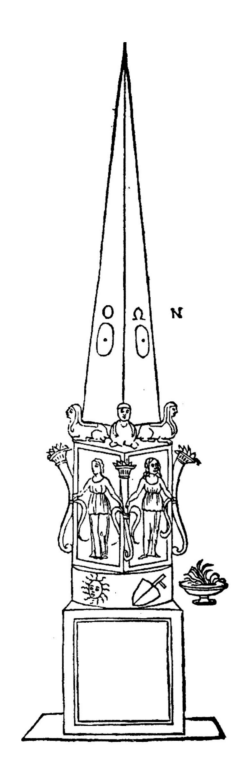

29. A MONUMENT TO THE DIVINE TRINITY

The two maidens, Logistica and Thelemia, led Poliphilus to another circular garden where he sees an areostyle arcade made of bricks, five paces high from the ground to the top of the arch and three in across, tiled to keep the rain on the outside.[55] The arcade was covered and overgrown with green ivy, leaving only small areas of the wall visible. A hundred or these arches enclosed a flower orchard; Poliphilus continued by saying that under each arch stood a golden statue of a divine-looking nymph on a base made of porphyry, each adorned differently from one and the other.

In the centre was what Poliphilus states as a "mysterious thing" [56]. There was a cubic base of translucent chalcedony. On this, within the square, was a cylindrical stone of red jasper, two feet high and a one and a-half pace in diameter.[57] Atop this and fitting with its circle, was a black triangular stone a pace and a half in height, whose three angles extended to the limit of the plinth beneath. One each of the faces of the triangle had an image with its feet resting on the part of the cylinder that was not covered by the triangle. These figures were as tall as the black stone to which they adhered; they extended their left and right arms to the angles, holding a cornucopia affixed to the dulled points, which were cut off by their fingers at a distance of one foot, two inches. The horns, ribbons and statues shone with pure gold and the hands were looped with loose and sinuous ribbons that seemed to fly through the surface of the stone, and they were dressed as nymphs.

On the flat, square faces of the lower figure, Poliphilus saw three hieroglyphics: the sun, an antique rudder and a dish containing a flame.

Above each angle of the dark stone, Poliphilus saw a four-footed gold Egyptian monster. The first had a human face, the second half-human, half-beast and the third was bestial. Above this, seemingly rising from the backs of these creatures, was a gold three-sided prism, five times as high as its lower face or diameter. Each face of the prism was carved with a plain circle, above which was a Greek letter (O, N, Ω).

Logistica explained that the figure illustrated celestial harmony and that the significance of these hieroglyphs was the following message: "To the Divine and Infinite Trinity, One in Essence."[58] The lower figure was consecrated to the Divinity, because it is produced from unity and measures one on every side. It is the primary foundation of the other figures; the circle around it has no beginning or end. The sun represents power over everything, that is, God. The rudder represents infinite Wisdom and the dish containing a flame represents Love. Each is single, yet joined.

Logistica also explained to Poliphilus that the creatures beneath the golden obelisk represent "three great and famous opinions"[59] and because the human form predominates, so do the opinions of the human. The three elements of time – past, present and future – are represented by the circles on the pyramid. The circles are arranged in a way to symbolize that no person can clearly see any time but the present.[60]

Logistica explains to Poliphilus that the primary, transparent figure at the base is known only to itself. Someone "endowed with intelligence will ascend and…consider the coloration of the second figure."[61] She continues by declaring that someone who searches further will arrive at the third figure, which is dark and surrounded by golden images. Poliphilus is then given an enigmatic conclusion, which is as mysterious as the monument itself: *the person who climbs higher will still find a figure of triple forms, which rises and tapers to a point.* "Here even the best informed can learn no more than that the thing is," Logistica says, "but as to what it is, they remain ignorant, impotent and incompetent."[62]

When Logistica completes her philosophical lesson and after Poliphilus marvels at the mysterious obelisk, the "curious thing" one last time, they hold hands with each other and with Thelemia, embark on a journey toward the three doors described before by Queen Eleutirillide.

PLATES

PALACE AND GARDENS OF
QUEEN ELEUTIRILLIDE (LIBERTY)

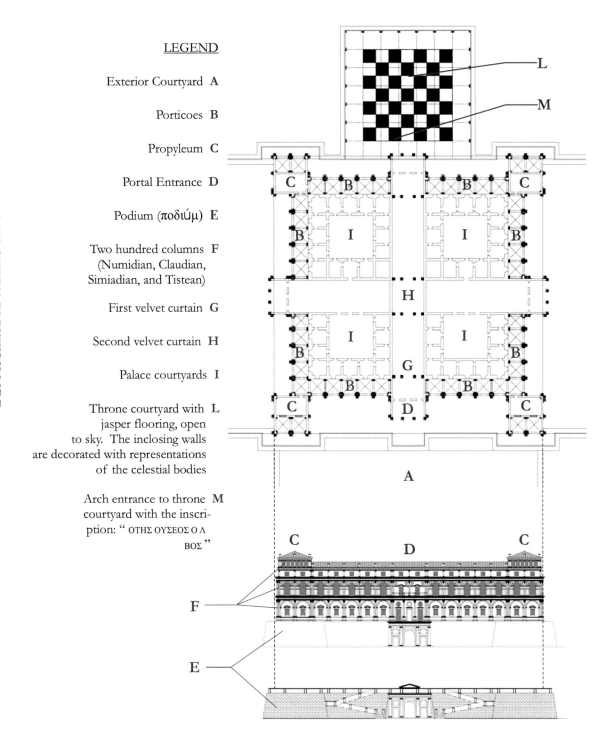

<u>LEGEND</u>

Exterior Courtyard **A**

Porticoes **B**

Propyleum **C**

Portal Entrance **D**

Podium (ποδιύμ) **E**

Two hundred columns **F**
(Numidian, Claudian,
Simiadian, and Tistean)

First velvet curtain **G**

Second velvet curtain **H**

Palace courtyards **I**

Throne courtyard with **L**
jasper flooring, open
to sky. The inclosing walls
are decorated with representations
of the celestial bodies

Arch entrance to throne **M**
courtyard with the inscription: " ΟΤΗΣ ΟΥΣΕΟΣ Ο Λ
ΒΟΣ "

PLATE I

FAÇADE AND PLAN DRAWINGS
OF THE
MAIN VILLA COMPLEX

LEGEND

Entrance **A**

Main courtyard **B**

Fountain with three nymphs **C**

Main palace complex **D**
with courtyards & porticoes

Courtyard of the queen's throne **E**

Garden of glass **F**
(*Viridarium*)

The Garden of silk **G**

Tower & entrance to the **H**
labyrinth of water canals

Labyrinth of water canals **I**

The rotunda pavilion with a **L**
"...*cupula di virgule doro
cum mulpiplici & florigeri rosarii
ricoperti...*"

The round colonnade of **M**
one hundred columns
(displuvium)

Three-sided obelisk monument **N**
of the celestial harmonies
(DIVINAE INFINITAEQVE
TRINITATI VNIVS ESSENTIAE)

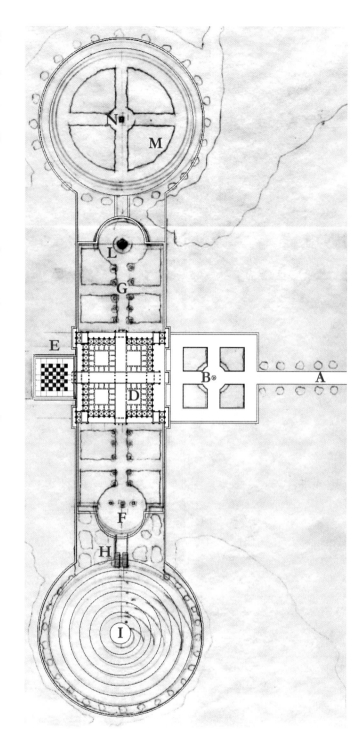

PLATE II

PLAN RECONSTRUCTION
OF THE
VILLA & SURROUNDING GARDENS

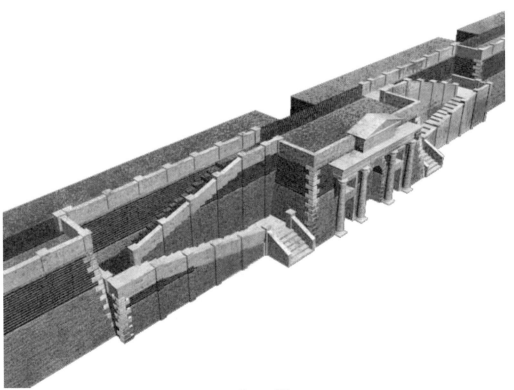

PLATE III

MAIN PERSPECTIVE VIEW
&
DETAIL OF THE PODIUM

ΕΛΕΥΘΕΡΑ

PLATE IV

PRONAO ENTRANCE & PODIUM

PLATE V

PERSPECTIVE VIEW FROM
MAIN COURTYARD ENTRANCE

PLATE VI

PERSPECTIVE VIEWS OF THE PROPYLAEUM

PLATE VII

PERSPECTIVE VIEW OF
MAIN FAÇADE & COURTYARD

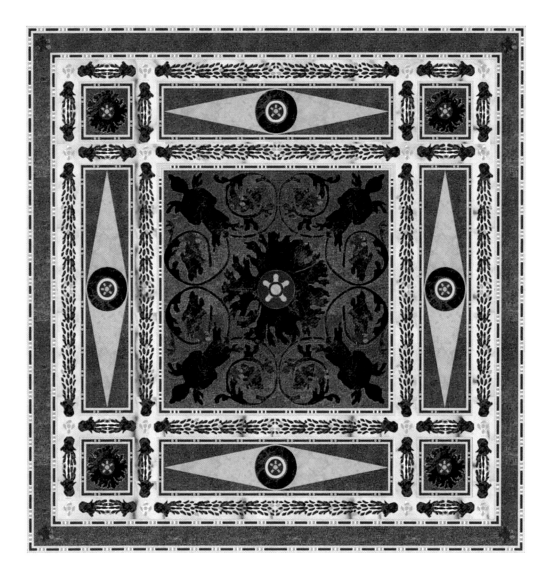

PLATE VIII

MATERIALS: MARBLE POLYCHROME & MOSAIC
FLOOR AT MAIN COURTYARD

Synnadic Marble

Claudian Granite

Plate IX

MATERIALS: COLUMNS

126

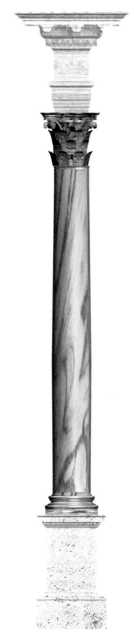

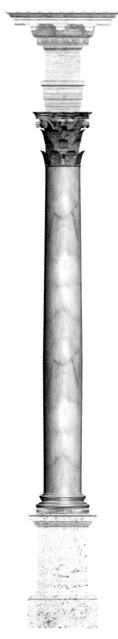

CARYSTEAN MARBLE   NUMIDIAN MARBLE

PLATE X

MATERIALS: COLUMNS

PLATE XI

ELEVATION OF THE PROPYLAEUM

PLATE XII

MAIN PERSPECTIVE VIEW
(ENLARGED)

DIVINAE INFINITAEQUE TRINITIATI VNIVS ESSENTIAE

PLATE XIII

MAIN ELEVATION & PLAN OF THE
MONUMENT TO THE DIVINE TRINITY

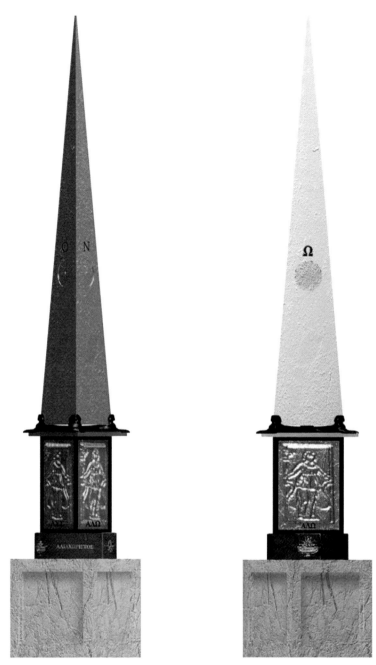

NORTH & WEST SIDE   SOUTH & EAST SIDE

PLATE XIV

ELEVATIONS OF THE
MONUMENT TO THE DIVINE TRINITY

LEGEND

Three sided obelisk of gold **A**

Circular incision **B**

Inscription of three Greek **C**
letters O, N, Ω each distributed
on three sides

Three sphinxes with **D**
different heads: a human,
half-feline, and completely
feline, representing the sub-
division of the soul

Prism of "blackest" stone **E**
with "graceful" and "divine"
nymphs in gold

Cylinder made of red jasper **F**
with three different
hieroglyphs representing
the eternal cosmos with the
inscriptions: ΑΔΙΗΓΗΤΟΣ, ΑΔΙ
ΑΧΩΡΣΤΟΣ, ΑΔΙΕΡΕΓΝΗΣ

Four-sided base made of **G**
translucent calcedony with the
inscriptions: ΔΥΣ Α ΛΩ ΤΟΣ

According to Poliphilus' companion,
Logistica, this monument praises
homage to the "*divine and infinite
trinity of the prime essence*"

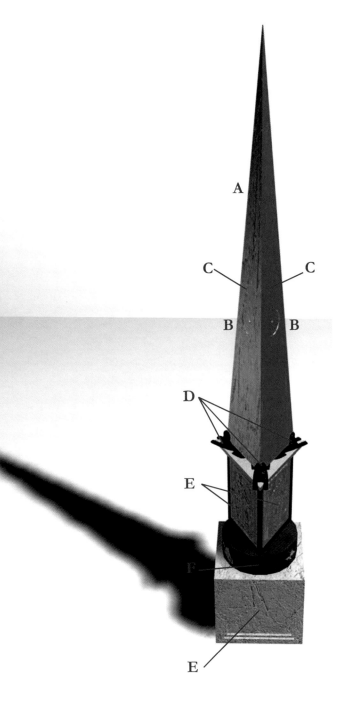

PLATE XV

AXONOMETRIC VIEW OF THE
MONUMENT TO THE DIVINE TRINITY

PLATE XVI

PERSPECTIVE VIEW OF THE
MONUMENT TO THE DIVINE TRINITY

PLATE XVII

PERSPECTIVE DETAIL OF THE
MONUMENT TO THE DIVINE TRINITY

PLATE XVIII

PERSPECTIVE VIEW OF THE BASE & THE PRISM

PLATE XIX

PERSPECTIVE VIEWS OF THE
MONUMENT TO THE DIVINE TRINITY

PLATE XX

PERSPECTIVE VIEW OF THE
QUEEN'S THRONE COURTYARD

PLATE XXI

ANGLE VIEW OF THE
QUEEN'S THRONE COURTYARD

PLATE XXII

WIDE PERSPECTIVE VIEW OF THE
QUEEN'S THRONE COURTYARD

PLATE XXIII

BIRD'S EYE VIEW OF THE
AQUATIC LABYRINTH

PLATE XXIV

VIEW OF THE MAIN TOWER
AND ENTRANCE GATE

PLATE XXV

VIEW OF THE AQUATIC LABYRINTH
TOWARDS THE MAIN PALACE COMPLEX

Plate XXVI

THE AQUATIC LABYRINTH:
INTERIOR PERSPECTIVES

PLATE XXVII

THE AQUATIC LABYRINTH:
EXTERIOR PERSPECTIVES

PLATE XXVIII

AQUATIC LABYRINTH:
FAÇADE OF THE MAIN TOWER

CHAPTER SIX

THE TEMPLE TO VENUS PHYSIZOA

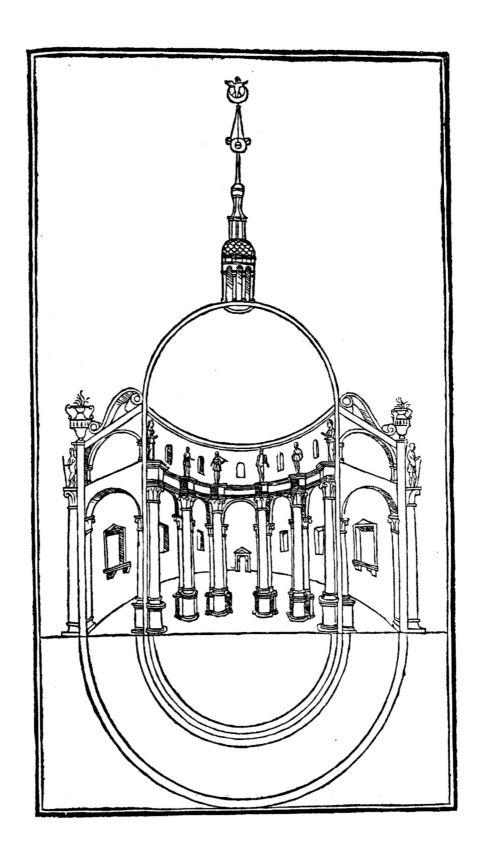

30. THE TEMPLE TO VENUS PHYSIZOA

"...*O infœlici tempi & ætate nostra, come dagli moderni (usando coveniente vocabulo) si bella & dignifica inventione, e ignorata? Per la quale cosa imaginare alcuno non se debbi, che Trabi Phrygii, coronamenti, base, capitelli, columne, columne semi. Pavimento, crustati, Alamento, coassatione, & tutta la comaginatione, Dimensione, Partitione, se accusasseron sencia inditio degli solerti & præstanti ingenii antiqui & orisci exquisitamente excogitati & digesti...*"

"...Oh, how unhappy is our own time and age, when the moderns (to use the convenient term) are ignorant of so beautiful and worthy invention! No one should image that beams, friezes, coronas, bases, capitals, columns, half-columns, pavements, plaster work, walls, floor joists, and all the joints, dimensions, and partitions can be laid out without an inkling of how the eminent and skillful geniuses of antiquity and early times studied and understood them..."

- *Poliphilus, as he describes the Temple of Venus Physizoa.*[1]

P OLIPHILUS, CONTINUES ON A DELIGHT-FILLED JOURNEY WITH many nymphs and he is torn between his lusty desires and his devotion to his true love. After a celebration held around a sacred altar, Poliphilus discovers that one of the nymphs is his beloved Polia, who leads him to the Temple of Venus Physizoa[2]. Finally reunited with the woman of his dreams, Poliphilus is amorous and, yet, he seems more entranced by a man-built structure.

Although he follows Polia around like a "led beast," he takes "voluptuous pleasure" in his surroundings and his "eyes escaped a little from their sweet captivity and bondage"[3] to spy what seemed to be a high rounded turret above a rounded roof in the distance. His attention strays with unnatural swiftness away from the nymph of his obsessions and toward the beauty of this temple instead.

Poliphilus describes a high dome, which he thought was roofed in grey lead, topped with an octagonal cymatium with columns and another dome. Above this dome were eight square pillars covered with a roof in baluster shape and atop this was a pinnacle with a shiny round sphere. Poliphilus moved away from Polia for a closer inspection of the structure. He is introspective enough to wonder about his priorities, his fascination "for this thing which drives me with such sharp and constant longing…[and] would make me contented above any lover."[4] As it may seem hard to believe, at least for now, Poliphilus' love of architecture triumphs over love for a woman.

ARCHITECTURAL COMPOSITION:

The temple consecrated to Venus Physizoa is described by Poliphilus as a rotunda, inscribed within a square figure on the ground (ABCD, fig. 31). The diameter of the rotunda was the same length as the height of the square. There was also another square (GHIF, fig. 31) drawn within the circle ("X", fig. 31) created by the base of the rotunda. In Poliphilus' vision, the space between one of the sides of the rotunda and its circumference was divided into five parts with a sixth added near the centre ("M", fig. 31). Poliphilus noticed that it was the architect's intention to create a round building between two circles ("X" and "Y", fig. 31).

In fact, the architect in Poliphilus' vision draws ten radii from the centre to the outer circumference, and the lines determine the ten arches, which rest on serpentine columns that formed the interior circular wall. Standing two feet[5] out from the interior wall was a polished Corinthian column made of clear porphyry. Each Corinthian

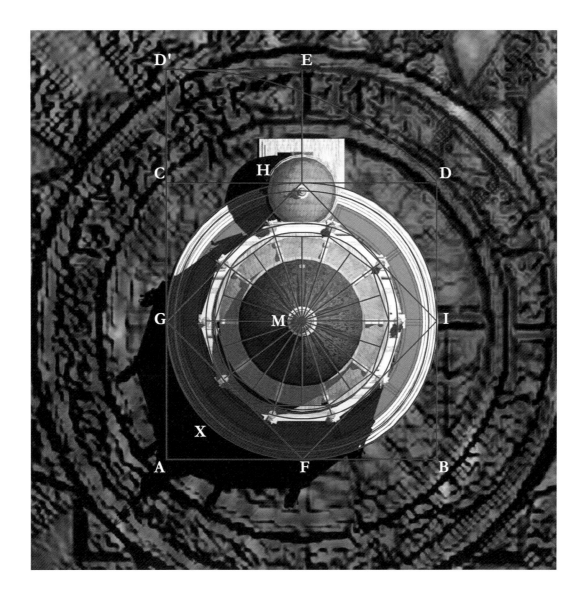

31. BIRD'S EYE VIEW OF THE TEMPLE & PROPORTIONS

column, nine diameters in height, not counting the bronze capital, stood on an alabaster half-cylinder-shaped base. These were attached on either side to half-pedestals, formed by taking two squares, each the width of the lowest diameter of the column. Poliphilus compares the height of the column to that of the Ionic order[6]. The capital itself supported a horizontal beam that followed the curved, central wall, which was previously described.

The bases and capitals were composed of shining refined bronze. Poliphilus applauds the architect for the design, which included porphyry columns standing on their own pedestals and connected to the pillars but with openings in the intercolumniation to increase the amount of floor space. [7]

The ends of the curved beams rested on the smooth, polished serpentine columns. Each end descended to a slab on top of the capital, where below, there was a half altar. The half-altar assumed the role of pedestal for the bases of the serpentine columns.

Poliphilus continues by mentioning that the central arches were decorated with putti, shells and foliage. Inside the triangles formed by the arches were roundels of jasper, framed by gilded foliage

A fluted square pilaster (made from the same serpentine) protruded from the pillar of the arch behind the Corinthian columns, with its square protruding in an amount equal to a third of its width. They were decorated with candelabra, leaves, fruits, flowers and birds, with its outside face having a frame. The base of the pilasters meet with similar bases and pedestals attached to the wall beneath the adjacent arches. It seemed to Poliphilus that the space between the arches was the result of the radii drawn to the circumference when aligned with the outermost pillars.

32. THE TEMPLE TO VENUS PHYSIZOA

(FRENCH EDITION)

The half-cylinders and semi pedestals (that defined the central space) were decorated with curving, leaf garlands and various fruits. Eight rectangular windows with their panels made of very thin Bolognese foil,[8] were positioned between the square-fluted pilasters of the outside wall. It seemed to Poliphilus that these windows were carved out of the empty space between the pillars, in the space beneath the curves of the arches. He observed that the arches were equidistant from the pillars as the distance from the first exterior cornice that ran around the first roof

Poliphilus also describes zodiac mosaics as wainscoting, beneath the windows, depicting the months of the year as well as the phases of the moon and orbit of the sun, the passing of seasons, and finally, the winter and summer solstice. He guesses the mosaics might have been designed by Petosiris, a famed mathematician, or by Necepso, due to the accuracy of these ingenious representations.[9] He was most impressed, saying they "had a laudable and joyful effect on the senses of the soul." [10]

The other walls of the temple were inlaid with precious marbles and various symbols. A sculpture of Apollo sitting and playing his lyre was placed above the order of one of the Corinthian columns. Above each of the other columns, composed of a single piece of stone, was a Muse in different gestures and poses.

The universal symmetry of the work pleases Poliphilus, who praises the "illustrious architect" who designed it. In the centre of the temple, he finds something else that pleases him: a crystal lantern above the alabaster cistern that was sustained by a system of pure gold chains and rings. Poliphilus describes the lantern to have four chains, which are attached to an inverted shell at the top by hooks. The four equal chains held a circular plate about midway between the top shell and the bottom lantern. The bowl of the lantern, made of pure crystal and "hollowed to a degree of thinness that

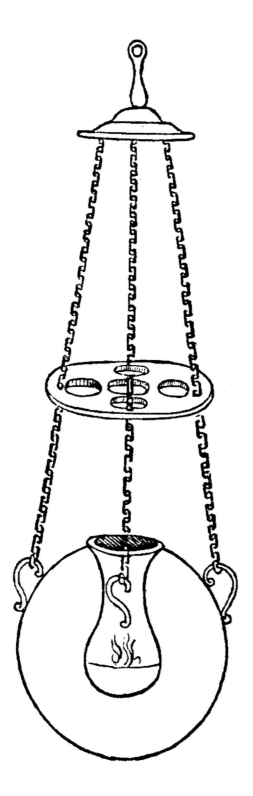

33. The Temple to Lantern

could not be achieved on the lathe"[11] contained a gourd-shaped vase inside an opening that was half an arm-length in diameter. The vase was carefully inserted, Poliphilus observed, so that the light of the lamp would shine in its centre.

Poliphilus raved about the "miraculous" floor finishes that were superior to the pavement of Zenodorus in Pergamum,[12] and the mosaic of the Temple of Fortune in Praeneste.[13] The floors of the temple were made of the finest porphyry and serpentine stones cut into tiny mosaics, creating rings that framed ten roundels. Each of the roundels was composed of a particular colour and type of stone, which measured a foot across. They included red jasper, lapis lazuli, green jasper veined with chalcedony and agate. The flooring beneath the arched "portico" of the temple was made of tiny mosaics of cut stone that had been evenly polished or carved.

EXTERIOR ARCHITECTURE:

There were ten pillars and ten arches on the outer wall (minus the bay to which a chapel was attached). Poliphilus describes the pillars projecting from the exterior (those beyond the square columns attached to the first circuit of walls):

* The projection of the pillars equalled the thickness of the wall.

* The distance between the pillars was determined by dividing the radii.

* By dividing the radii, one portion was for the breath of the pillar. The other portion was again divided, with each of these half portions (or quarter portions of the radii) allowing for a pilaster on either side. These pilasters provided structural arches to the solid wall as well as blind arches between each of the pilasters.

* Poliphilus recognizes the projection of the pillars divided into three parts. One part would be the protrusion of the arch from the surface of the curved wall. Two parts would be taken up by the protrusion of the two small pilasters.

* The exterior wall, arches and pilasters were all composed of the same solid pieces of stone made from Augustian marble and alabaster, joined together without ironwork.

* The same cornice joined the temple and adjacent chapel (whose roof, which had a closed dome that was distinct and free from the larger dome of the temple, was built above the cornice).

The largest dome included workmanship "more nearly divine than human":[14] from a single casting of metal gilded in pure gold were carvings of vases arranged perpendicularly above the columns. The vases were filled with branches and intricate tendrils and around them were scenes of infants plucking grapes, flying birds, lizards and snakes. Viewed from the ground, Poliphilus noticed that the scenes appeared normal in size.

The outside pillars were made consistently with the rest of the building's architectural design. The footing of these pillars was encircled by a band of toruses, fascias, gullets and quarter-circles, which corresponded to similar characteristics inside the sanctuary; the actual columns themselves were made from majestic porphyry topped by Corinthian capitols.

Poliphilus noted that the design of the building also created an efficient water-drainage system. This was made possible by a hollowed-out channel along the exterior wall, that met the slope of the roof so that when it rained, the water trickled down the roof to the channel and then down the drain pipes inside the exterior porphyry pillars to the ground, flowing into a cistern, which was located at the centre of the temple and was sculpted of alabaster including a choir of nymphs carved around it, in relief. The excess of water was quickly drained away, leaving enough for ritual use.

On the roof, Poliphilus found inserted between the dome and the exterior wall, a "…volute or scroll shaped covering made from two contrary spirals. One curled downwards touching the dome, while the other curled upwards in the shape of a snail shell, touching the [exterior porphyry] pillar…"[15] Above this exterior pillar stood a "…candelabrum of lustrous orichalcum whose mouth opened like a shell, in which an inconsumable material was burning with an inextinguishable flame…these miraculous candelabra looked uniform in their proportions and of equal height, with suitable handles…" [16]

Poliphilus sees on top of the cupola eight little pilasters. Their height was the proper height of two squares and there was an inverted ewer with its mouth open above them. Poliphilus observes that all the elements of this elevation was "exquisitely measured and mathematically proportioned." [17]

The base of the ewer, which defined the pinnacle of the dome, was roofed with seed-shaped tiles and held a hollow ball that had been fused to it. Poliphilus deduced that the bottom of the ball had been pierced in four places to prevent ice formation that would have limited its function as a bell. The spire rose from the centre of the ball and tapered to a sharp point above which was a bronze moon "as wide as it looks on its eighth day, with its horns (pointed) to the sky,"[18] which provided a perch for an open-winged eagle. [19] Four bronze chains were hanging from hooks attached to the spire beneath the moon; each held at its end a brass bell. These bells, which had comb-like

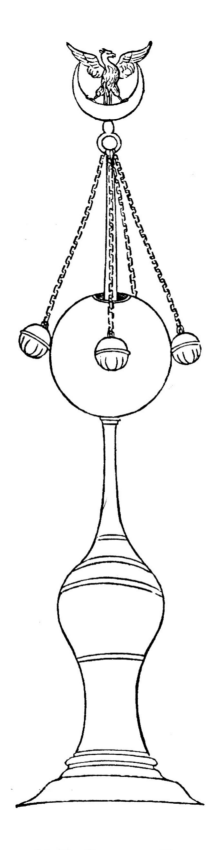

34. THE BELLS OF THE TEMPLE

fissures from the middle to the bottom, enclosed a bead of fine steel and produced a tinkling sound when they struck the hollow ball.

Poliphilus concludes his observations of the temple with a description of the entrance, which, he said, was made from fine jasper in the Doric tradition. A Greek inscription, "ΚΥΛΟΠΗΡΑ,"[20] was inscribed in pure gold above the entrance's fascia. The doors of the temple were decorated with bright metal and piecework, which opened by themselves through a system of "magnets." A plate of polished steel was attached on the doors' interior. Tablets made from Indian lodestone and encased next to the openings of the door on the inside of the temple, which provided the magnetic pull. Not merely functional, the lodestones also bore inscriptions. The right quoted Virgil "*Trahit sua quemque voluptas*" (let each follow his own pleasure), and the left bore the Greek inscription "ΠΑΝ ΔΕΙ ΠΟΙΕΙΝ ΚΑΤΑ ΤΗΝ ΑΥΤΟΥ ΦΥΣΙΝ (let each do according to his own nature).[21]

Poliphilus, torn as usual between ancient architecture and present temptation, pauses in his exploration of the temple to return his attention to "the incredible beauty of the divine nymph who captured my gazing eyes and possessed my whole soul."[22]

35. Doors for the Temple's Entrance

PLATES

THE TEMPLE OF VENUS PHYSIZOA

PLATE I

PERSPECTIVE SECTION VIEW OF THE TEMPLE

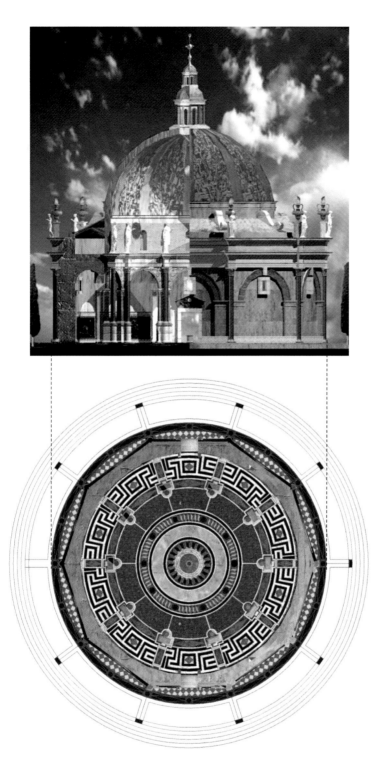

PLATE III

FAÇADE / SECTION AND PLAN VIEW

PLATE III

EXTERIOR ARCHITECTURAL VIEWS
WITH SURROUNDING GARDENS

PLATE IV

EXTERIOR ARCHITECTURAL DETAILS

PLATE V

INTERIOR ARCHITECTURAL VIEWS

PLATE VI

INTERIOR ARCHITECTURAL VIEWS

PLATE VII

INTERIOR ARCHITECTURAL DETAILS

PLATE VIII

LARGER EXTERIOR PERSPECTIVE

PLATE IX

EXTERIOR PERSPECTIVE AND
SIDE ELEVATION WITH CHAPEL

PLATE X

BIRD'S EYE VIEW OF THE
TEMPLE & CHAPEL

POLYANDRION:
CEMETERY OF LOST LOVES

36. Poliphilus Amongst Ancient Ruins

"...Ove pensiculatamente coniecturai questo essere stato magnifico, & meraveglioso templo di eximia, & soperba structura. Secundo che la proba & perclara nympha scitulamente ad me vaticinato havea...."

"...Oh, I conjectured, after some thought, that this had been a magnificent and marvelous temple of rare and superb construction, just as the virtuous and excellent nymph had aptly prophesied to me ..."

- *Poliphilus, as he admires the remnants of what used to be the Polyandrion.*[1]

THE AMOROUS SPIRIT THAT HAUNTED THE TEMPLE OF VENUS had a profound effect on Polia, who partakes in a swan-sacrificing ceremony with the high priestess in a tribute to the divine. From the blood of the beautiful birds grows fruits and flowers, symbols of the young lovers' passion. Polia, demurring that they must continue to await Lord Cupid, distracts Poliphilus with the suggestion that, since he is "extremely fond of looking at the works of antiquity" [2] he should spend some time observing the near-by ruins of the cemetery of lost loves.

Poliphilus, "without another thought," leaves the seductive Polia to view the thorn-tangled, ivy-covered ruins. From what had been preserved of a round temple surrounded by a tribune[3], Poliphilus finds fragments of pillars, zophori, cornice and columns of assorted types of stone, including Numidian, Hymettian, and Laconic[4].

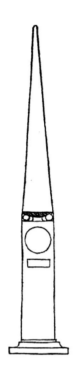

At the rear of the temple, Poliphilus finds a tall obelisk of reddish granite, [5] supported by a square base. Several hieroglyphs were carved on to its sides: a pair of scales, a dog and a serpent (fig. 38). Below the scales, a sword was risen from an antique coffer; its tip rose above the bar of the scales and through a crown at the top. The sword served as the centre support of the scales, the crown as an ornamental "bolt" that attached the middle support to the bars of the scale. Poliphilus interpreted the hieroglyph to mean: "Lawful justice, unsheathed and free from love and hate and well-considered liberality, firmly preserve the kingdom."[6]

37. OBELISK IN HONOUR OF
JULIUS CAESAR

38. HIEROGLYPHICS: "...LAWFUL JUSTICE...PEACE AND CONCORD ..."

39. HIEROGLYPHICS: IN HONOUR OF JULIUS CAESAR

Below this, Poliphilus sees another hieroglyph (fig. 39): an eye, two ears of wheat tied together, a scimitar, beribboned wheat-flails, a globe and a rudder in another rectangle. Within this rectangle, there also was a vase containing a fruit-adorned olive branch, a plate, six coins in a circle, an open-door chapel and two ibises. Poliphilus interprets this scene to be a tribute to Julius Caesar, erected by and paid for by the ancient Egyptians.[7]

On each remaining face of the square block, Poliphilus sees hieroglyphs inside carved circles (fig. 38). The first included serpents wrapped around a centre pole and, on either side of the rod, two elephants that diminished. From these picture-clues as well as a vase containing fire and a shell containing water, Poliphilus interprets the scene to mean, "Through peace and concord, small things increase, through discord, great ones diminish."[8]

40. Hieroglyphics: Strongest Bond of an Empire &
Caesar's Many Victories

Opposite to this side was another circle (fig. 40), which had a horizontal anchor with a spread-winged eagle resting on it and a rope wound around its shaft. A warrior surrounded by weapons and viewing a snake sits below the anchor. Poliphilus interprets this hieroglyph to mean that military discipline is the strongest bond of an empire[9]. On the fourth face (fig. 40), the encircled hieroglyph includes a trophy atop crossed branches. Above the trophy are horns and in the middle, there are two symbols: an eye and a comet. Poliphilus interprets this as a tribute to Caesar's many victories in battle[10].

After admiring the obelisk, Poliphilus returns to the ancient part of the temple. At the entrance of a broken doorway, Poliphilus finds a fallen beam, the zophorus and part of the cornice carved from a single piece. He notes that the bean fragment has retained its fine lineaments (fig. 41) with a description identifying the true name of

41. POLYANDRION: THE FRAGMENT OF THE ZOPHORUS

this monument as being a cemetery of lost loves[11]. He sees an alabaster headless bird and lamp. Although some portions of the carvings are missing, Poliphilus interprets the remains to mean, "Death-bearing messenger, to life." [12]

THE CIBORIUM AND THE UNDERGROUND HYPOGEUM

Poliphilus works his way through the debris to the centre of this roof-less temple (surrounded by what used to be a *tribuna*). Only one work had survived sufficiently enough to bear description. There was a six-sided ciborium[13] at the centre of this temple, which was made from reddish porphyry. It was set on a six-sided base of solid serpentine stone. Each of the six columns that rose from the base was set six feet apart. There were no lineaments on the polished epistyle, zophorus and cornice. The mouldings were angular on the outside, circular on the inside. A cupola, composed of a

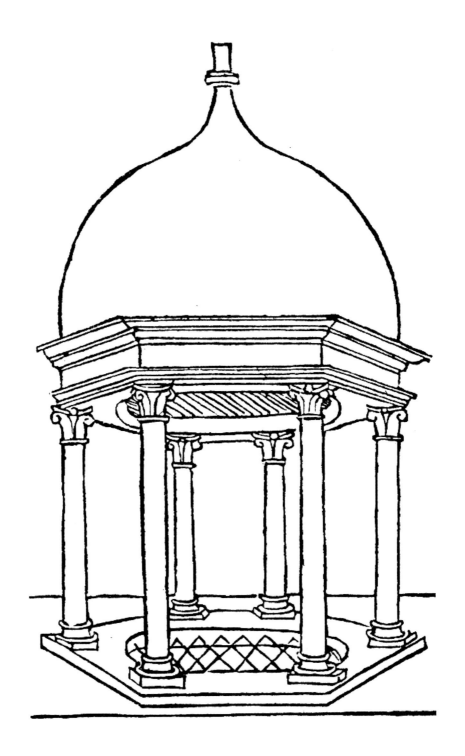

42. Ciborium

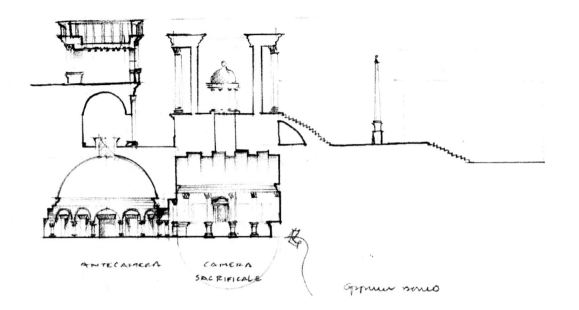

ANTECAMERA   CAMERA
              SACRIFICALE

Gypreum sonio

43. Study Sketch of the Hypogeum Below the Ciborium

single solid rock, rose above the corona and tapered upward to a narrow and hollow chimney. The cupola covered from what Poliphilus first observed to be an underground rectangular cavity in plan, covered by a cast metal grille that lay at the centre of the serpentine base below the columns of the ciborium. Insatiably curious, Poliphilus finds a way to descend into the cavity via a dark stairway he found near-by. Dark and gloomy, the stairway seemed to lead Poliphilus into nothing more than a damp, horrible hole. But once he reaches the bottom, he finds a spacious hypogeum, with an area hollowed out in a circle. It was supported by piers placed below the superstructure of the cupola, with its arches spanning openings equal to the size as those contained by the six columns above-ground. The area was vaulted from the piers upward, and the polished marble blocks were cemented together so carefully that the joints were nearly invisible.

On the floor between the piers was a double-square altar, six feet long and six feet high, including the base and cornice. The altar was hollowed out as a tomb. Poliphilus sees a small window, which he believes might have enabled the sacrificers to tend the fire and remove ashes when the sacrifice was concluded (fig. 44). From what he observes, he believes animals to be sacrificed were placed on top of a grille, set aflame with the smoke that can rise through the channel of the porphyry cupola so that the burning smell could quickly escape the temple "…as in the Egyptian rite…"[14]

44. Study Collage of the Hypogeum Below the Ciborium

A Decorative Mosaic Piece in the Tribune

Still underground, Poliphilus searches for other architectural splendours, finding none except seats joined to the walls. He returns to the surface and surmises that the temple holding the ciborium had an open roof even in antiquity, based on its preservation and after observing the adjacent, nearly intact tribune.[15] On a portion of the ceiling of this tribune, he sees a mosaic. Poliphilus notices that it represented a dark, fog-shrouded cavern which on one side had a decorated vault, and on the other side, a hollowed-out, storm-eroded mountain of *tufa*[16] stone. He continues by saying that between the two was a double bridge. Everything between the rocks seemed to be on hellish fire. Poliphilus calls it "a place of searing heat, full of fiery flying sparks running about and glowing ashes falling like dense atoms in the sun's rays and crackling in the flames." [17]

Also depicted in the front was a dark, muddy, frozen lake. To the right of this was a volcanic mountain. Amid the wrath of the Furies, wretched souls tried valiantly to save themselves. But the heat from the volcano scorched rather than warmed those in its vicinity and those who sought refuge in the coolness of the lake found freezing pain from the ice instead. The reason for this condemnation? Poliphilus reads an adjacent inscription that said that "…souls condemned to the burning flames were those who had killed themselves because of overheated love." Spirits plunged into the ice had been "…frigid and unyielding in matters of love..." [18] Love too much or too little in life, and you will reap eternal punishment in death; this, Poliphilus believed, was the message the artist intended to deliver.

HEV SVIATOR PAVLVLVM INTERSERE. MANIB. ADIV
RAT. PRODITVM. AC LEGENS POLYSTONOS METAL
LO OSCVLA DATO ADDENS . AH FORTVNAE CRVDE
LE MONSTRVM VIVERE DEBVISSENT. LEONTIA PVEL
LA LOLII INGENVI ADVLESCENT . PRIMARIA AMORIS
CVM INTEMPERIE VRGERET . PATERNIS AFFECTA
CRVCIATVB. AVFVGIT. INSEQVIT. LOL. SED INTER AM
PLEXANDVM A PYRATIS CAPTI INSTITORI CVIDAM
VENDVNT. AMBO CAPTIVI NAVEM ASCEND. CVM NO
CTV SIBI LEONT. LOL. AVFERRI SVSPICARET. ARREP.
TO GLADIO NAVTAS CVNCTOS TRVCIDAT. NAVIS
ORTA MARIS SAEVIT. SCOPVL. TERRAM PROPE COL
LISA MERGIT. SCOPVL. ASCEND. FAMIS IMPVLSV LE
ONT. HVMERIS ARRIPIENS IMPONO. FAVE ADES DVM
NEDT. PATER INQVIENS. NOS NOSTRAMQ. FORT. TI
BI COMMITTO. TVNC DELPHINEO NIXV BRACHIIS SE
CO VNDVLAS, AT LEONT. INTER NATANDVM ALLO-
QVIT. SVM NE TIBI MEA VITA MOLESTIAE? TI PVLA LE
VIOR LEONT. CORCVLVM, ATQ. SAEPICVLE ROGANS
SVNT NE TIBI VIRES MEA SPES. MEA ANIMVLA? AIO.
EAS EXCITAS, MOX COLLVM AMPLEXATA ZACHARI
TER BAIVLANTEM DEOSCVLAT. SOLAT. HORTAT.
VRINANTEM IN ANIMAT. GESTIO. AD LITT. TANDEM
DEVENIM. SOSPITES. INSPERATO INFREMENS LEO, AG-
GREDITVR, AMPLEXAMVR INVICEM, MORIBVNDIS
PARCIT LEO. TERRITI CASV, NAVICVLAM LITTORI V
NA CVM REMIGA LIPAL MICVLA DEIECTAM FVGITIVI
ASCEN. VTERQ. ALTERNATIM CANTANTES REMIGA-
MVS. DIEM NOCTEMQ. TERTIAM ERRANT. IPSVM
TANTVM VNDIQ. COELVM PATET. LETHALI CRVCIA-
MVR FAME, ATQ. DIVTINA INEDIA TABESCENTIB.
RVIMVS IN AMPLEXVS, LEONTIA INQVIENS AMABO
FAME PERIS? SAT TECVM ESSE LOLI DEPASCOR, AST IL
LA SVSPIRVLANS MI LOLI DEFICIS? MINIME INQVAM
AMORE SED CORPORE. SOLIS VIBRANTIBVS ET MV-
TVIS LINGVIS DEPASCEBAMVR DVLCITER, STRICTI-
VSQ. BVCCIS HIANTIBVS OSCVLIS SVAVE INIECTIS HE
DERACITER AMPLEXABAMVR, AMBO ASTROPHIA
MORIMVR, PLEMMYRIIS NEC SAEVIENTIB. HVC AVRA
DEVEHIMVR, AC AERE QVAESTVARIO MISERI IPSIS IN
NEXI AMPLEXVB. MANES INTER PLOTONICOS HIC SI-
TI SVMVS, QVOSQ. NON RETINVIT PYRATICA
RAPACITAS NEC VORAVIT LEONIA IN-
GLVVIES, PELAGIQ. IMMENSITAS
ABNVIT CAPERE, HVIVS VRNVLAE
ANGVSTIA HIC CAPIT AMBOS,
HANC TE SCIRE VOLEBAM
INFOELICITATEM.
VALE.

45. Epitaph to the Lovesrs Leonzia & Lolio

As Poliphilus left this area, he found a squared marble stone that was damaged on one side but otherwise largely intact. On one of its faces was a central section that contained two small squares with an arch. On each side of the arch was an oval figure. Above the head of one figure was the letter "D" and above the other was the letter "M"[19]. On top of this was a pointed, truncated cyma and above this an open vase that Poliphilus surmised might have been meant to hold ashes.[20] Nearby, a tablet of porphyry was lying on the ground, inscribed by an epitaph dedicated to a gladiator by his lover. This discovery leads to another: an altar on which an old man was holding the head of a goat by its horns. Nearby, resting against a tree, a man dressed in goat-skins, is playing two flutes. A naked infant dances between the man holding the goat head and the man playing the flutes. On the other side of the altar was a man carrying a large wine vessel on his shoulders while, behind him, a naked woman holds a torch. Behind this pair was a satyr child who held a coiled snake in his hand and a peasant-woman carrying a basket of fruits and leaves on her head. The peasant carries a long-necked vase in her other hand.[21]

Poliphilus leaves this site and returns to the broken tribune where he sees another bright mosaic, this one depicting a woman prostrating on a burning pyre while slaying herself. There was an altar in the tribune, but it was badly in ruins. Nearby was an antique vase, a pace and a half in height, made of alabaster stone. One of the vase's handles was missing the body of the vase was slightly broken. The vase rested on a plinth and bore an inscription.[22]

At another ruined tomb, Poliphilus reports seeing a mosaic depicting a youth (Lolio) swimming with a girl (Leontia) on his back to a deserted shore. Poliphilus could also see part of a lion and two persons rowing a boat but the rest of the mosaic had been destroyed. Each inscription tells a story, and Poliphilus is saddened by the assorted tributes to departed loved ones, which included the story of these two lovers who had died of hunger[23]. Moving away from the inscribed altars, Poliphilus finds two preserved corpses and two coronets inside a tomb inscribed with hieroglyphs including glass bottles, pottery vessels, and an antique metal lantern and another epigraph that told a story of unfortunate lovers. A different sort of man might have wanted to leave the cemetery and its dismal tales, but Poliphilus is inspired by the sights and encourages himself to return to his beloved Polia for the potential of a happier ending. Instead, "feeling ever more enthused," he continues his explorations and finds another ruined tomb located in the tribune.[24]

THE MONUMENT OF THE QUEEN OF CARIA

This tomb, which retained its right-hand wall, included two small squared columns protruding from the edges of the wall by a third of their width. A pedestal stood perpendicular to and beneath the columns. Mourning nymphs turned, weeping, toward the centre, where an inscription in Greek gave the identity of the person whose memory is immortalized: "ΑΡΤΕΜΙΣΙ ΔΟΣ ΒΑΣΙΛΙΔΟΣ ΣΓΟΔΟΝ"[25]. An ornate epistle extended beyond the two capitals. The zophorus, decorated with leaves with flowers, was above the epistle and over the zophorus was a corona.

Poliphilus continues his description: There was a throne between the two square pilasters. Four equally-spaced lion's paws supported an antique trunk on the inside floor of the niche. A stool covered with fringed silk sat on the lid of the trunk. A majestically cloaked queen sat on this throne, holding a chalice to her mouth with one hand and a

46. TOMB OF THE QUEEN OF CARIA

sceptre in her left. The queen wore an indented crown and a coronet with points atop hair that was pulled into a half-bun, with the remaining hair cascading down her back. An image of the king's head, held by two nude spirits, is above the keystone of the arched beam that enclosed the queen. Each of the spirits, sitting on the arch, held the king's head in one hand while holding onto a string of branches and berries with the other.

Over the cornice and an ornamented, slightly sloped plinth, was a circle of metal that encircled a black stone inscribed with Greek letters[26]. A nude statue, holding a spear in its right hand and an antique shield in its left, stood on top of the circle. Two nude putti flanked the circle at its bottom, each holding a light torch. Slightly below and toward the outer edges, two nude, winged infants sat on top of the cornice. In one of their hands, the infants held fruit. They each had another arm wrapped around an ancient brass candelabrum that looked like a vase with dolphin handles.

All of this sat on a base of square serpentine that rose from the pavement. Most of the base was free of lineament, but there was a maritime carving in the middle. This included the prow of an ancient ship. At its centre was a tree trunk, with military cuirass that hung from its branches. Other objects, asymmetrically placed, included an anchor, a collar and a crested helmet.

OTHER TOMBS OF THE CEMETERY

Nearby, Poliphilus found another elegant tomb. Most of the stone was reserved for an epitaph but above this was a "portrait" of the two lovers. The carving showed two nude boys drawing back a curtain to reveal the heads and upper torsos of a man and maiden in courtship finery. Another monument included two fluted columns at the edges, "carved in the half-round from the solid stone of whitest marble, with bases, capitals, beam, zophorus, cornice and pediment."[27] Inside the triangle formed by the pediment were two doves drinking from a small vase. Below this, Poliphilus could see two doorways of a coffer with nude children going into one and out the other. Poliphilus reasoned from the inscription that this representation symbolized the circle of life: when we exit one portal by dying, we enter another portal that leads to the afterlife. The coffer itself stood on two harpy's feet that turned into foliage.

Poliphilus leaves the site "with joy and gratification"[28] and hurries to see a half-standing tomb that included a mosaic but no sarcophagus that he could find. The mosaic showed Proserpina with Cyane and the Sirens picking flowers off a burning Mount Etna, while Pluto had unleashed the flames of the volcano, abducting Prosperina to satisfy his loving urges. About this time, Poliphilus was suddenly startled by falling *tesserae.* The cause turns out to be a wall lizard, and when Poliphilus ceases to be frightened by reality, he replaces his fears with the thought that his Polia will suffer a fate similar to the woman in the mosaic. Determined that his own love story not end as tragically as the ones he has been immersed in, Poliphilus flees the cemetery, his "eyes bedewed with tears," and hastens into the welcome arms of Polia.

PLATES

POLYANDRION:
THE CEMETERY OF LOST LOVES

LEGEND

Propylaeum where Poliphilus **A**
discovers the architrave with
the inscription:
"D.M.S. CADAVERIB.
AMORE FVRENTIVM
MISERABVNDIS POLYANDRION".

The *tribuna* **B**
where tombs are located.

Obelisk in Egyptian red granite **C**
inscribed with hieroglyphics
praising Julius Caesar, with curious
messages.

A roofless circular temple **D**
with a *ciborium* in solid red
porphyry in the center.

The *ciborium* made of porphyry **E**
with six columns over a hexagonal
base in serpentine stone
with a grill covering an opening
leading to a sacrificial *hypogeum* below
as in the "ancient Egyptian manner".

Columns **F**
(Numidian, Hymettian,
Laconic, and "others").

Square leading towards the **G**
epitaphs of lost loves.

Entrance to Polyandrion from **H**
first floor level.

Ground floor level **I**

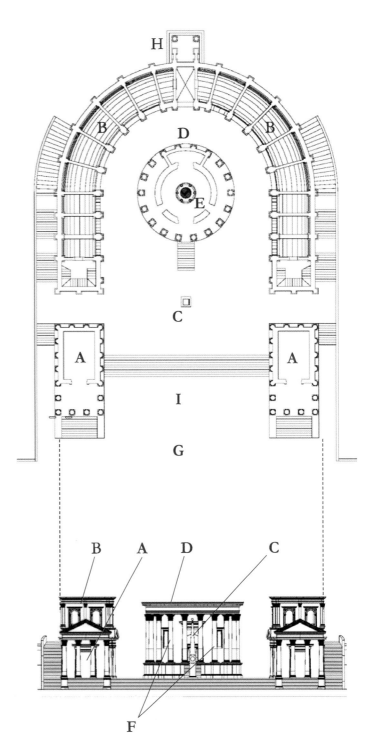

PLATE I

PLAN AND ELEVATION OF THE POLYANDRION

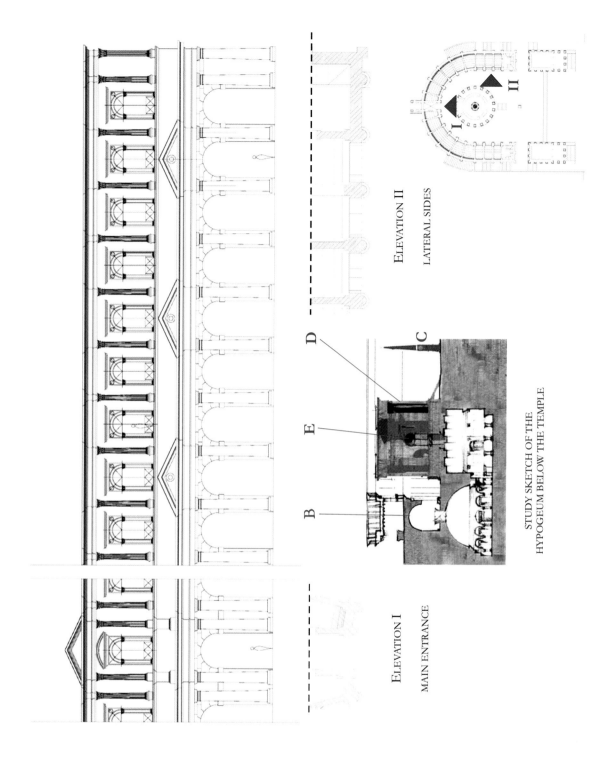

ELEVATION II
LATERAL SIDES

I

II

D

C

E

B

STUDY SKETCH OF THE
HYPOGEUM BELOW THE TEMPLE

ELEVATION I
MAIN ENTRANCE

PLATE II

ELEVATION STUDIES OF THE TRIBUNA
AND THE HYPOGEUM

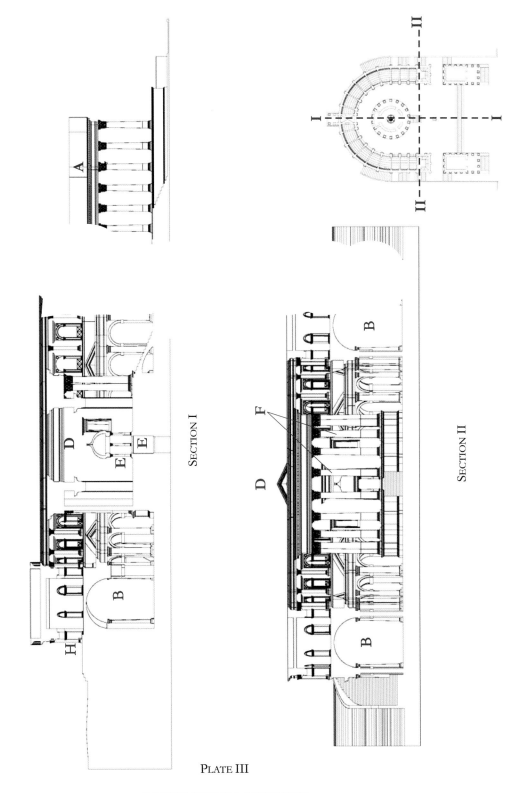

SECTION I

SECTION II

PLATE III

POLYANDRION: SECTIONS

PLATE IV

PERSPECTIVE & BIRD'S EYE VIEW OF THE MAIN TEMPLE COMPLEX

PLATE V

PERSPECTIVE VIEWS OF THE CIRCULAR TEMPIETTO AND PROPYLAEUM

PLATE VI

PERSPECTIVE SIDE VIEWS THE PROPYLAEUM AND TRIBUNA

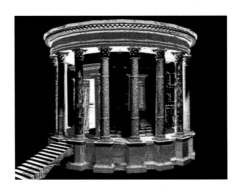

PLATE VII

DETAILS: OBELISK, TEMPIETTO, AND CIBORIIUM

PLATE VIII

SECTION: THE MAIN TEMPLE COMPLEX

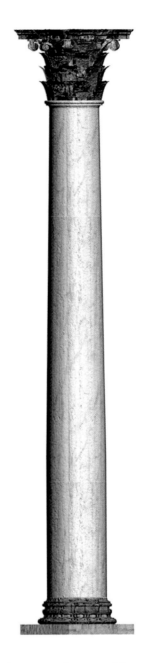

GIALLO ANTICO MARBLE

NUMIDIAN ANTIQUE MARBLE

PLATE IX

MATERIALS: COLUMNS

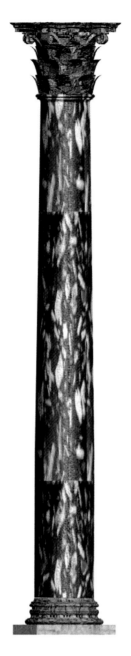

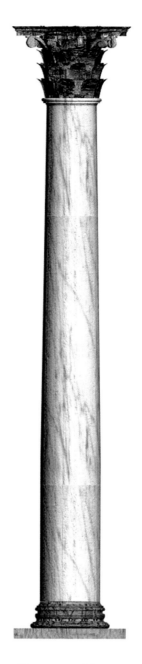

LACONIC MARBLE
FROM SPARTA

HYMETTIAN MARBLE

PLATE X

MATERIALS: COLUMNS

RED PORPHYRY COLUMNS
EPISTYLE, ZOPHORUS, & CORNICE

SERPENTINE OR *OFITE*
MARBLE BASE

PLATE XI

MATERIALS: CIBORIUM

FRONT SIDE   LATERAL SIDES   BACK SIDE

PLATE XII

MATERIALS: OBELISK / RED THEBAN GRANITE

NOTES

*

INTRODUCTION

1   It is no surprise that the *Hypnerotomachia* has contributed greatly to landscape architectural design, and that samples can be seen in Italy such as: the gardens of Villa d'Este in Tivoli (near Rome), the famous Boboli gardens near Florence, and the relatively recent "Scarzuola" Gardens (near Orvieto, Italy) by Tommaso Buzzi in 1956 (just to name a few). Emanuela Kretzulesco Quaranta has also suggested in her book, *Les Gardins du Songe, Poliphile et la Mystic du Renaissance* (Paris, 1986), that the design for the famous Versailles gardens had some inspiration from the text, p.326-327.

2.   Already discovered as early as the 16th century, the following acrostic reads by placing the first letter of each chapter in sequential order: *POLIAM FRATER FRANCISCUS COLUMNA PERAMAVIT* (Brother Francesco Colonna deeply loved Polia). Based on this discovery, contemporary scholars have identified two potential "authors" born 20 years apart: Francesco Colonna, an unruly Dominican Monk who lived in the monastery of SS. Giovanni e Paolo in Venice, or a Roman Prince who came from a powerful feudal land-owning family, whose roots, they claimed, go back to the Julio-Claudian Caesars. The Roman Colonna's uncle, Prospero, was also an active member of the renaissance humanist "*Accademia*" of Pomponio Leto in Rome, which leads to the possibility that young Francesco was also a member of this "collegiate society" (colleagues of these secret congregations usually referred to each other as "brother," which can explain the acrostic). Lefaivre, has recently argued Leon Battista Alberti as a plausible author due to certain similarities in literary expression, not to mention his impeccable knowledge of classical languages and literature, painting, sculpture, the building arts, engineering, perspective, etc. Alberti was also hired as a consultant to "restore" the Colonna family's palace in Palestrina near Rome, which provides a direct link to Francesco and the humanist "*accademia*"

(Liane Lefaivre, *Leon Battista Alberti's Hypnerotomachia Poliphili. Re-Cognizing the Architectural Body in the Early Italian Renaissance* (Cambridge, London, 1997). Nevertheless, the vast amount of archeological, historical, architectural, linguistic, and philological information incorporated in the *Hypnerotomachia*, would seem too much for just one person to write about. It would be interesting to consider the possibility that the "*Accademia*" of Pomponio Leto itself was the author, and that it was *a group effort*. In my opinion, this hypothesis is highly probable considering that key individuals such as power struggling aristocratic figures in Roman and European politics, humanist scholars, practicing professionals (artists, architects, etc.) were all active members of this society, and that they were united in reviving the culture and wisdom of Classical Rome and Greece (which is repeatedly evident in Poliphilus' narrative).

For more information on the Venetian Francesco Colonna, please refer to M.T. Casella e G. Pozzi, *Francesco Colonna. Biografia e oper*, 2 Vols (Padua, 1952). For more information on the Roman Francesco Colonna as a plausible author, please refer to Maurizio Calvesi, *Il Sogno di Polifilo Prenestino (Rome*, 1980), and E. Kretzulesco-Quaranta, *Les Jardins du songe: Poliphile et la mystique de la renaissance* (Paris, 1976).

3.   For more information on the virtual reconstruction of historic Bologna, please refer to the following articles published in the "History and Computer Science Dept." section of the University of Bologna website: http://www.storiaeinformatica.it/nume/en glish/ntitolo_eng.html:

o   Francesca Bocchi, "The New *Electronic* Museum (NUovo Museo Elettronico) - The City in 4 Dimensions: Virtual Bologna" in *Nuove metodologie per la storia delle città: La città in quattro dimensioni*, from *Medieval Metropolises, Proceedings of the Congress of Atlas Working Group* (Bologna, 1999), 11-28.

*

o   Fernando Lugli, Esteban Cruz, "Technical notes - Modeling no longer existing buildings. Virtual reconstructions based on information in the 1294 *Liber terminorum* [Bologna Center]" in *Methodology/Modeling/Building Reconstruction – Technical Notes* [present on the same website].

CHAPTER 1

1.   A Parisian, baroque painter who was commissioned to realize the following works of art depicting Poliphilus' *Hypnerotomachia* early in his career:

  o   "*Poliphile au bain des nymphes*" (1643) at the Magnin Museum, Dijon, France. Poliphilus along with his nymph companions enjoy the Queen's baths.

  o   "*Le Dieux marins rendent honneur a l'Amour*" (1643) at the J.P. Getty Museum, Los Angeles. Poliphilus and Polia during their boat escape towards the Island of Citera from the Ancient Port.

  o   "*Poliphile ayant choisi la porte d'Amour est accueilli par Philtronia*" (1643) at the Residenzgalerie, Salzburg. Poliphilus must choose one of the three doors (God, worldly greatness, or Love) that his companions (Logistica and Thelemia) present him; he chooses Love, of course.

  o   "*Poliphile assist au triomph de Bacchus*" at the Musee de Tesse (1643, Le Mans). Poliphilus witnesses the triumph of Bacchus.

  o   "*Polilphile s'agenouille devant la reine Éleuthérilide*" (1643) at the Musee des Beaux-Arts, Rouen, France. 1643. Poliphilus kneels before Queen Eleutrillide, swearing his allegiance.

2.   Silvia Fogliati e Davide Dutto, *Il Giardino di Polifilo: ricostruzione virtuale dalla Hypnerotomachia Poliphili di Francesco Colonna stampata a Venezia nel 1499 da Aldo Manuzio* (Milan, 2002).

3.   Hieroglyphics in the *Hypnerotomachia* are Renaissance "interpretations" of ancient Egyptian inscriptions (noting that "real translations" were not provided for until after the discovery of the Rosetta Stone by Napoleonic forces during their Egyptian expedition in 1798). Fascination with Egyptian hieroglyphics in the Renaissance probably began after Cristoforo Buondelmonti (a Florentine traveller and merchant) who, in 1422, brought back to Florence, an ancient Greek manuscript from the island of Andros, entitled *Hieroglyphica* by Horapollus (circa 5th century BCA). Mario Andrea Rigoni, *I Geroglifici, Biblioteca Universale Rizzoli* (Milan, 1996), p.5. This re-discovered work was an instant success, after its first modern publication in 1505, in Venice by the same Aldus Manutius of the *Hypnerotomachia*. The nature of the original text by Horapollus was only allegorical or symbolic, and not an exact "translation" of Egyptian hieroglyphics. It was however, the only classical recourse available until the discovery of the Rosetta stone two centuries following.

4.   A few sample sketches are included in the "Plates" section at the end of this chapter. These samples represent most of the monuments that have been included in this publication with the exception of two gardens of the Queen Eleutirillide, her Bath, the Hypogeum and Epitaphs which are present in the Cemetery of Lost Loves (Polyandrion), an Ancient Port City, and finally the Island of Citera. All of these monuments are currently under study and development. A few schematic sketches have been presented here as an introduction to the work.

5.   Maurizio Calvesi, *Il Sogno di Polifilo prenestino* (Rome, 1980), 57-62, 66-135.

6.   Emanuela Kretzulesco-Quaranta, *Les Jardins du Songe. Poliphile et la Mystique de la Renaissance* (Paris, 1986).

7.   Liane Lefaivre, *Leon Battista Alberti's* Hypnerotomachia *Poliphili: Re-Cognizing the Architectural Body in the Early Italian Renaissance* (Cambridge, 1996).

*

8. Stefano Borsi, *Polifilo architetto: Cultura architettonica e teoria artistica nell'Hypnerotomachia Poliphili di Francesco Colonna, 1499* (Roma, 1995).

9. Francesco Colonna, *Hypnerotomachia Poliphili* (Padua, 1980), Vol. I-II, translation into the Italian and comments by G. Pozzi, L.A. Ciapponi.

10. See endnote n. 14

11. Francesco Colonna, *Sueño de Polífilo* (Barcelona, 1999), comments and translation in the Spanish by Pilar Pedraza.

12. Leon Battista Alberti, *De Re Aedificatoria* (Milan, 1989), translation in the Italian by Giovanni Orlandi with comments and notes by Paolo Portoghesi.

13. Marcus Vitruvius Polio, *De Architectura Libri X* (Padova, 1990), translation in the Italian by Luciano Migotto.

14. Francesco Colonna, *Le Songe de Poliphile*, translation into the French by Jean Martin (Paris, Kerver, 1546), presentation, transliteration, notes, glossary, and index by Gilles Polizzi (Paris, 1994).

15. Francesco Colonna, *Hypnerotomachia. The Strife of Love in a Dreame* (London, 1592), translated into the English by R.D., a facsimile reproduction of the Longleat copy and introduction by Lucy Gent (London, 1973).

16. Francesco Colonna, *Hypnerotomachia Poliphili: The Strife of Love in a Dream* (from now one indicated as HP-Godwin), translation and introduction by Joscelyn Godwin (London, 1999).

17. Francesco Colonna, *Hypnerotomachia Poliphili*, translation into the Italian and comments by Marco Ariani and Mino Gabriele (from now on indicated as HP), Vol. I-II (Milan, 1998), 32, 36. While stupefied after observing with care the great Pyramid dedicated to *Occasio* or Fortune, Poliphilus confesses his admiration for the ancient architect who designed this massive structure saying that "…[the Pyramid] *teniva in se tanta cumulatione di miraveglia, che io di stupore insensate stava alla sua consideragione. Et ultra molto piu la immensitate dill opera, & lo excesso dilla subtigliecia dil opulente & acutissimo ingiegnio, & dilla magna cura, & exquisite diligentia dil Architecto…*" while continuing with emotion "…*sono sicuro di non avere la capacità do descriverla compiutamente, sopratutto perchè ai nostri tempi termini originali, stabiliti dai nostri padri e peculiari all'architettura, sono estinti e sepolti con I grandi del passato. O esecrabile, ampia barbarie, come hai potuto profanare e spogliare la parte più nobile del pregioso tesoro, il sacro recinto della latinità e l'arte un tempo così onorata, ora scelleratamente oscurata e offesa dalla perfida ignoranza? Ignoranza che, accoppiata a una spasmodica, insaziabile e malvagia avidità, ha accecato proprio quella somma e divina arte che fece di Roma l'ineguagliabile signora del mondo…*" For the English translation, HP-Godwin, 25, 30.

18. Ibidem, 57-58. For the English translation: Ibidem, 42-43.

19. Interestingly, Lefaivre points out innovative and creative architecture described in the *Hypnerotomachia*, and quotes Alexander Tzonis when explaining the ways architectural creativity works (and how this mechanism is evident in Poliphilus' descriptions on architecture): "…new design ideas are born, not ex-nihilo but out of the recombination of precedents. By bringing together precedents in an unprecedented way, creative design uses memory and knowledge as a basis for innovatively combining elements." Lefaivre, L. *Leon Battista Alberti's Hypnerotomachia Poliphili: Re-Cognizing the Architectural Body in the Early Italian Renaissance* (Cambridge, 1997), 46.

20. Lefaivre comments that the description of the Queen's palace is quite innovative for its time, by saying that "…the building is the first display of color in western writings about architecture…" Ibidem, 53.

21. This reference is completely literary, cited from Giulio Capitolino's "Vita Gordiani" in *Historia Augustae*: "…*est villa eorum via*

NOTES

*

Praenestrina duecentas columnas in tetrastylo habeas quarum quinquaginta Carystae, quinquaginta Claudianae, quinquaginta Synnadae, quinquaginta Numidicae pari mensura sunt..." HP, 137.

22. Hanno-Walter Kruft, *Geschichte der Architekturetheorie: Von der Antike bis zur Gegenwart* (Munich, 1985), translated into the English by Ronald Taylor Elsie Callander, and Antony Wood (New York, 1994), 73.

23. HP, 92-93. Infact, Poliphilus is quite stunned as to the magnificence of the site when saying *"...Ero assolutamente convinto che il geniale architetto fosse stato il più bravo fra quanti mai hanno edificato. Quale armatura di travi e puntoni, quale ordinata disposizione di stanze, camere, cortili, quali muri coperti e rivestiti di preziosi tavolati, quale mirabile sistema di ornamentazione, quale ininterrotta sequenza di coloratissime pitture sulle pareti, qale ordine e ritmo dei colonnati...davanti a questo splendido colonnato con le sue duecento colonne numidiche, claudiane, simiadi e tistee equamente distribuitte. Che marmi, che sculture...quale propileo, quale vestibolo, quale regale portico...si aggiunga inoltre la magnificenza degli ordini delle finestre, dell'imponente portale, del nobilissimo podio, alte espressioni dell'arte edificatoria..."* For the English translation, please refer to: Francesco Colonna, *Hypnerotomachia Poliphili: The Strife of Love in a Dream*, translation and introduction by Joscelyn Godwin (London, 1999), 92-93.

24. Hanno-Walter Kruft, *Geschichte der Architekturetheorie: Von der Antike bis zur Gegenwart* (Munich, 1985), translated into the English by Ronald Taylor Elsie Callander, and Antony Wood (New York, 1994), 73.

25. Ibidem, 72-79. It is interesting to note that most of the architectural treatise produced in the *Quattrocento* was destined for a particular audience: patrons and clients of architects. The needs of architectural practitioners following Alberti were never truly addressed until the publication of Sebastiano Serlio's eight books on architecture and the building arts after 1537. As a designer, I considered these theoretical

works carefully while comparing any of his elaborations to architectural details or similarities implied in the *Hypnerotomachia*. This of course was only the case when dealing exclusively with "visionary" architecture or what Giulio Romano would say a generation later, *"...anticamente moderna e modernamente antica..."* (G. Vasari, *Le Vite de' più eccelenti pittori scultori architettori nella redazione del 1550 e 1560*, Vol. I-IV, Florence, 1927, curate by Rosanna Bettarini, with secular comments by Paola Barocchi). Considering that his treatise was published only 38 years after the *Hypnerotomachia*, Serlio's work was very helpful with initiating simple architectural concepts when addressing the façades, plan, and courtyard strategies, as well as architectural detailing solutions.

CHAPTER 2

1 HP, Vol. I, 25. HP-Godwin, 25.

2 Ibidem, 22. HP-Godwin, 22.

3 According to Ariani and Gabriele's commentaries, this description of using "argilla rossa" or "red clay" between the joints of large stone block construction (as a substitute for mortar) comes directly from Leon Battista Alberti's classic, "On Building" (De Re Aedificatoria), where he describes this technique evident in ancient Roman examples. HP, p.548. After reviewing Godwin's translation (maybe "too literal"), this detail can be confusing because the joints are not "painted red", instead the joints are "pointed in red clay" as is described in the original Italian *(...& tāto exquisitamente rubricati gli sui lymbi...)*, HP p.22. As a confirmation, the original source is found in: Leon Battista Alberti, On the Art of Building in Ten Books, translated by Joseph Rykwert, Neil Leach, and Robert Tavernor (Cambridge, 1999), 75: "...those who have noticed that when big stones are used in ancient buildings, the joints are pointed in red clay, have suggested that it was being used as a mortar..."

4 Ibidem, 22. HP-Godwin, 22.

NOTES

*

5   Ibidem, 22. HP-Godwin, 22.

6   Most of this work on the Pyramid complex was based on detailed descriptions by Poliphilus. In some cases of ambiguity however (such as the interior lighting system or the stairway leading to the top), it was necessary to "design" or complete the pyramid's components and composition because our narrator only mentions their existence without any tangible reference to their architectural arrangement. For clarity concerning significance, classical reference, measurements, and materials, Ariani/Gabriele's commentaries were quite helpful during reconstruction. HP, 565-580.

7   HP, 25. HP-Godwin, 25.

8   Sacred mountain in Greece, legendary home to the Greek pantheon of deities.

9   The Base of the Pyramid: Equivalent of 1.137 meters or 3.570 English feet. The height of the base including the great cornice: the equivalent of 36.9 meters or 115.87 English ft. high.

10   HP, 28. HP-Godwin, 28.

11   In this allegory, Poliphilus is referring to the Roman god of war battling with two other titanic figures of Greek mythology: Porphyrio and Alcyoneus. Porphyrio was a ferocious giant who was one of the offspring of Uranus and Gaia. This monster is known to have attempted rape to Hera (the wife of Jupiter, father of the Roman pantheon of deities). Alcyoneus (also known as the "mighty ass") was a γίγαντας (gigantes), or one of the titans who sprang forth from the blood of the wounded Uranos after being castrated by Kronos (the father of Zeus, king of the gods). They were known to threaten constantly Mt. Olympus, which was the legendary keep of the gods in Greek mythology.

12   The resulting super-structure reached a summit at a height of 1,410 cubits high,

which in modern equivalents would be 923 meters or 2,898 English feet.

13   HP, 24. HP-Godwin, 24.

14   Equivalent to 6 meters or 18.84 English ft.

15   HP, 24. HP-Godwin, 24. Equivalent to 3 meters or 9.42 English ft.

16   Ibidem. Equivalent to circa 21 meters or 66 English ft.

17   Ibidem. Equivalent to circa 21 meters or 66 English ft.

18   According to commentaries by Gabriele and Ariani, the tintinabulum was a bell that was wrung during Roman times to sign the hour for bathing. Another interesting note by the commentators refers to the "five Pyramids". This is another allegory taken from Leon Battista Alberti and Pliny: the legendary Porsenna had a labyrinth built in the form of a square, with five pyramids positioned above it. At it's summit, a bronze disk with "tintinabula" were installed so that their ringing could be heard after large distances. HP, p. 564

19   HP, 25. HP-Godwin, 24-25.

20   It is interesting to note that Poliphilus' description of the interior of the Pyramid has a similarity with Boullée's architectural theories (i.e. Cenotaph to Newton of 1784, Cenotaph for Turenne, and funerary architecture, 1760-1799). In fact, Lefaivre also suggests how the Pyramid in the Hypnerotomachia surpasses any architectural known standards of its time: "This is one of the most daring floutings of an established architectural "no" in the book, not only because the chamber is so immense…but because of its utterly naked walls. This radical rejection of ornament is unique for the Quattrocento." Lefaivre, L. *Leon Battista Alberti's Hypnerotomachia Poliphili: Re-Cognizing the Architectural Body in the Early Italian Renaissance* (Cambridge, 1997), 47. Interestingly enough, Boullée, like Alberti, claimed that architectural forms derive from natural ones. Pérouse de

Montclos, J.M. *Etienne-Louis Boullée, 1728-1799* (Milan, 1997), 144, 277.

21 HP, 27. HP-Godwin-27.

22 HP, 28. HP-Godwin-28.

23 "ΛΙΧΑΣ Ο ΛΙΒΥΚΟΣ ΛΙΟΘΟΔΟΜΟΣ ΩΡΘΟΣΕΝ ΜΕ" My translation: The Libyan architect Lichas built me. Ibidem.

CHAPTER 3

1 HP, 30-31. HP-Godwin, 30-31

2 Ibidem.

3 HP, 31.

4 HP-Godwin, 31. This rather emotional reference expressed by Poliphilus is an example of how the Roman past is glorified and remembered through the memory of her antiquities, which is one of the reasons why Calvesi suggests a Roman Prince Colonna as a plausible author, since this family constantly held a "propaganda war" with papal authorities emphasizing their classical, ancient ancestry.

5 In modern equivalents, 14.9 meters or 46.8 English feet.

6 The diameter where the horse's hoof covered was 1.48 meters, or 4.6 English feet, with the distance from the hooves to the underside of the belly to be 2.67 meters, or 8.4 English feet.

7 According to Gabriele and Ariani's commentaries, it is interesting to note that parsley was an herbage noted by the ancients especially Virgil, as being appropriate to decorate crowns for giving tribute to a victory. The addition of fennel gives a superlative, bitter quality to the already bitter companion previously noted (HP, p. 588) . Could it be that this ambiguity, along with the Latin title, alludes to misfortune?

8 Underlined by Gabriele and Ariani, ancient scholars gave significance to this herb as

damnation. According to Ovid, if Venus did not approve of someone's love, anyone who refused her approval was candidate for receiving a dose of aconite (HP, p.589).

9 A legendary green marble from Sparta, Greece. HP, 595.

10 HP, 37. HP-Godwin, 37.

11 Poliphilus describes the obelisk to be one pace wide at the base (1.47 m / circa 4.62 ft. circa) and 7 paces high (10.30 m / 32.34 ft).

12 HP, 595-596. According to the curators, this semi-transparent material could be a metaphor for the human *mens* or spirt-intellect by quoting Pliny when describing what is at the top of emperor Augustus' obelisk incorporated in his meridian: "...*aurata pila...ratione...capite hominis intellecta...*"

13 In modern equivalents, 17.64 meters long or 55.4 English feet circa, 7.35 meters wide or 23 English feet, and 4.4 meters high or 13.85 English feet.

14 Poliphilus describes this vision in detail: The first statue was a crowned figure of a man made of dark stone with silver detail work while in the position of standing on a tomb sarcophagus. It held in one hand a scepter, and in the other, a shield, which was inscribed with Hebrew, Greek, and Latin to say "...I would be nude, if the beast would not have covered me. Seek and you will find. Leave me..." The second statue was similar to the first one, however instead of a man, was a figure of a queen pointing its index figure behind it. As in the first example, it held a shield, however with the following inscription in the same languages: "...Whoever you are, take as much as you want of this treasure. But beware: take away the head, but do not touch the body..." According to Calvesi, the allegory of the queen and the black king may have an alchemical significance. Calvesi, M. *Il Sogno di Polifilo prenestino* (Rome, 1980), 86.

*

15 HP, 40. HP-Godwin, 40.

16 My translation: "…With your labor, you sacrifice freely to the god of nature, gradually, humbly offering to God your soul. By governing with compassion, He will firmly protect your life to be unharmed…" Ibidem, 41.

17 Modern equivalents: 89.4 meters or 280.7 English feet.

18 There is an entire section of the *Hypnerotomachia* dedicated to the Colossus that Poliphilus describes in detail. Resembling a middle-aged man with features that one cannot help but remind of the famous Hellenistic sculpture, Laocoön and his sons (140 B.C). Within the superstructure of this monument, Poliphilus describes that he finds all the organs, tissues, bones, and other biological morphologies sculpted with their names chiseled in Latin, Greek, and ancient Chaldaean. Included in the descriptions were allusions to sickness, ailments, and diseases along with their cures and remedies. Refer to HP, 41-42 or to HP-Joscelyn, 35-36.

CHAPTER 4

1 HP, 42. HP-Godwin, 42.

2 For easier reference, the reader can make reference to elevation number "1" on PLATE III – PROPORTIONS, P.87.

3 HP, p.42. HP-Godwin, 42. There is no doubt that this methodological explanation of the portal's proportions is "Albertian" in nature! In fact, Poliphilus mentions in the same paragraph "…*Questa figura di cordicelle quanto si præsta utile & opportuna ad reportare acurto, segmento, overo in lepturgia & in pictura in prompto se offerisce…*" This reference to using "threads" or *corda* (meaning "line") as a useful way for delineation in painting and intarsia work, is also mentioned in Alberti's *De re aedificatoria*, when quoting "…the architect…takes his projections from the ground plan and, without altering the lines

and by maintaining the true angles, reveals the extent and shape of each elevation and side…" Alberti, L.B., *On the Art of Building in Ten Books* (Cambridge, 1999), 34.

4 "Rhombus" is a classical, geometrical term referring to an oblique-angled equilateral parallelogram, in which Poliphilus' delineation can be seen on elevation number "3" on PLATE III – PROPORTIONS, P. 87.

5 As Ariani and Gabriele correctly point out, Poliphilus' frustration expressed here is obviously from Leon Battista Alberti when he condemns those who determine the aesthetics of a building without using any scientific or methodological fundamentals. HP, 631.

6 This obviously refers to the Golden Mean, which is an abstract method of proportion going back to Hellenistic times, however considered divine by Renaissance humanists. It consists of a line, which is cut in a way that the smaller section is related to the greater section, which then is related to the whole composition, by the proportion 5:8, approximately. This exercise was held very dear to Renaissance theorists, especially Leon Batista Alberti, when referring to his concept of *concinnitas* or "cosmic harmony." Since the Golden Mean is a recognition of nature by human observation, it is the desire of the Albertian architect to respectfully imitate nature, which by instinct emanates beauty: "…*La bellezza è accordo e armonia delle parti in relazione a un tutto al quale esse sono legate secondo un determinato numero, delimitazione, e collocazione, così come esige la concinnitas, cioè la legge fondamentale e più esatta della natura. La quale concinnitas è seguita quanto più possibile dall'architettura…*" Alberti, L.B. *L'Architettura* (Milan, 1989), 453. For the English translation and further descriptions, please refer to: Alberti, L.B., *On the Art of Building in Ten Books* (Cambridge, 1999), 302-309.

7 HP, 46. HP-Godwin, 46.

8 Ibidem.

9 Poliphilus' sermon on architectural practice, professional training, and ethics are obviously taken from Vitruvius' famous description: "…*Arquitecti est scientia pluribus disciplinis et variis eruditionibus ornate…Ea nascitur ex fabrica et ratiocinatione. Fabrica est continuata ac trita usus meditatione ad propositum deformationis, quae manibus perficitur e materia, cuiuscumque generic opus est. Ratiocinatio autem est, quae res fabricates sollertiae ac rationis proportione demonstrare atque explicare potest. Itaque architecti qui sine litteris contenderant, ut haberent pro laboribus auctoritatem ; qui autem ratiocinationibus et litteris solis confisi fuerunt, umbram non rem persecuti videntur. At qui utrumque perdidicerunt, ut omnibus armis ornati citius cum auctoritate, quod fuit propositum, sunt adsecuti….*" My translation : To determine the profession of the Architect, there are numerous disciplines that contribute…this science is the fruit of practical experience and theoretical fundamentals. Practice derives from continuous and insistent exercise finalized towards the realization of any construction that has been studied with care and precision in respect to its proportions. In case the Architect practices without any formal education, and only with practical experience, that professional will never be able to receive recognition in exchange for all the hard work contributed. On the other hand, for those who emphasis only on the theoretical aspects, they will never be able to realize any construction, but only its shadow. Instead, those who have a complete knowledge of both as if fully armed, will have attained their goal more quickly and with authority. Pollio, Marcus Vitruvius, *De Architectura Libri X* (Edizioni Studio Tesi, Padua, 1990), 7.

10 This reference is obvious for architects with regards to ethics in building and design: *Venustas, Utilitas, Firmitas*" (Beauty, Convenience [economy], and Durability) from Vitruvius: "…*[fora, porticus, balinea, theatra] autem ita fieri debent, ut habeatur ratio firmitatis, utilitatis, venustatis. Firmitatis erit habita ratio, cum fuerit, fundamentorum ad solidum depressio, quaque e material, copiarum sine avaritia diligens electio; utilitatis autem, (cum fuerit) emendata et sine inpeditione usus locorum disposition et ad regiones sui cuiusque generis apta*

et commoda distributio; venustatis, vero, cum fuerit operis species grata et elegans, membrorumque commensus iustas habeat symmetriarium ratiocinationes…" Ibidem, 28.

11 Poliphilus' delineation can be seen on elevation number "7" on PLATE III – PROPORTIONS, P.87 This entire proportion analysis, that Poliphilus overwhelms the reader with, most certainly is inspired from Alberti's system of methodological proportions: arithmetic, geometrical, and musical. The numerical progression that regulates the symmetry of the Great Portal is typical of the Albertian method of arithmetic analysis through geometrical means, within a rhythmical constant (hence, "harmonious" or "musical"). HP, 630.

12 HP, 46. HP-Godwin, 46.

13 This delineation can be seen on elevation number "11" on PLATE III – PROPORTIONS, P.87 Its description refers to squares "d, f1, g, f2, d" on this plate illustration.

14 With this particular description regarding the columns, there may be a slight confusion, which is evident comparing Ariani and Gabriele's modern Italian version with Godwin's modern English translation. According to the original Aldine text: "…*le due [colonne] vicino alla porta, di finissimo Porphyrite, & di gratioso Ophites, le altre due cariatice, overo striate, overo canaliculate…*", HP, 45. According to Ariani and Gabriele's translation: "…*quelle vicine alla porta erano della più nobile porfirite, mentre le altre due, di splendida ofite, erano striate e scanalate come la veste delle Cariatidi…*" HP, 61. Basically, the curators of the modern Italian version have clarified Poliphilus' specification for two *types* of columns used in the Great Portal's architecture (one type porphyry and the other, serpentine), in which one of these types (the serpentine) are fluted, or cut in the Cariatic style (fluted, similar to the "gowns of the Cariatids"). In addition, as the curators point out, the term *cariatice* or "Cariatic" is directly from Vitruvius. HP, 636. In contrast, Godwin's

*

translation reads "…The two columns next to the door were of finest porphyry and lovely serpentine; the other two were of Cariatic marble, furrowed or fluted…" HP, 45.

15 Also known as *"verde antique"*. For a closer description, please refer to Chapter 5, page 218, note n°19.

16 As indicated in note n° 14, above, "Cariatic" comes directly from Vitruvius. In book I of his treatise, when describing how the architect should have a thorough knowledge of history (to correctly recognize the significance of symbols used in a building's decoration), Vitruvius, as an anecdote, uses the example of an architect who must justify why caryatids were chosen instead of regular columns for his building: The use of caryatids originally refer to a tragic story related to the city of Caryae, of the Peloponnesus in ancient Greece. This city-state sided with the Greek's enemy, the Persians, during their war of occupation. After the Greeks were successful in defeating the enemy, the Hellenic hosts made the city pay for their treason by killing all of the men, and forcing their women into slavery, humiliating and enduring them to "bear the burden" for their former alliance. For this reason, the architects of that time incorporated statue representations of these poor souls as columns in order to remind the citizens of Carae the pain inflicted on their descendents. Pollio, Marcus Vitruvius, *De Architectura Libri X* (Edizioni Studio Tesi, Padua, 1990), 9-11.

17 This type of stone refers to Spartan stone used during classical times. It is also known as *porfido verde antico*, which is a deep green marble with white, crystal spots.

18 HP, 49. HP-Godwin, 49.

19 Ibidem, 49-50

20 Sard is a brownish chalcedony stone from Sardis, capitol of Lydia, in Asia Minor.

21 Ibidem, 46. For significance to Poliphilus' morale, please refer to note n° 9.

22 "Nothing Firm." HP, 49. HP-Godwin, 49

23 Ibidem.

24 Godwin's English translation reads: "…To the blessed Mother, the Goddes Venus, and to her Son, Amor, Bacchus, and Demeter have given of their own (substances)…" HP-Godwin, 51.

25 In Greek Mythology, Phoebus is non other than Apollo represented as a sun-deity. His nightly counterpart is obviously the moon (Phoebe), which is represented by Artemis (Diana). As a modern example of representation, a large fresco of these two can be seen today on the vault of the *Camera di Diana e Apollo*, Palazzo del Te (Mantua, Italy).

26 Leucothea is the mythological representation of the Morning. It is interesting to note that the same figures are also represented in Poliphilus' allegory in the opening chapter in the *Hypnerotomachia*, which seems to reinforce the argument presented in footnote, n° 28.

27 Daphne is the daughter of the Greek river god, Peneo. She was adored by Apollo, and she is frequently represented transforming into a laurel tree within a hair's grip from her lover. For artists of the Renaissance period, her theme was well known because she represented how chastity can overcome sensual and erotic love. It is interesting to note that Poliphilus finds a representation that is traditionally different from his contemporaries: Delos' advance, and her transformation as a sad one, and not a victory as it was popular to believe in his day among practicing artists.

28 According to Ariani and Gabriele's translation, this dedication would read: "to the Aegis of Jupiter." The commentators recognize that this allegory of the protective shield (made from the skin of the goat that fed Jupiter as an infant) along with the other erotic decorations of this *Magna Porta*,

*

is symbolic for the encouragement to Poliphilus to continue his quest through antiquity, notwithstanding the horrors of obscurity, since it was the same deity that encouraged him to resist when he was in the dark and gloomy forest, during the first part of his *Hypnerotomachia*. HP, 651-652.

29 Also known as *giallo antico*, which is an elegant, light marble from North Africa, and used in Roman times. For a graphical representation of this stone and other materials evident in the *Hypnerotomachia*, please refer to Chapter Five's Plates section.

30 See note n°17, P. 216

31 Europa, in Greek mythology, is the daughter of the king of the Phoenicians. Legend says that she was carried away by Jupiter (Zeus) in the form of a seductive bull, to Crete, where she bore him three sons: Minus, Sarpedon, and Radamanto. While ordered by his father to search for his sister in vain, Cadmo founds the legendary city of Thebes (which Poliphilus erroneously exchanges for Athens).

32 As the commentators Ariani and Gabriele suggest, the author is either wrong in mentioning Athens, or wants to re-invent the legend for some purpose. HP, 654. The critical reader of the *Hypnerotomachia*, however, wouldn't be surprised since this enigmatic text is full of blatant "no's" against established credence (see note n°20, Chapter Two, p. 212) possibly alluring to some message said "in-between-the-lines."

33 This passionate tale is also from Greek mythology: the famous Minotaur was the ferocious offspring of Pasiphae (wife of King Minus of Crete) and a bull sent by Neptune to her husband. As a punishment to Minus for not having sacrificed this animal to the deity, Neptune inspired Pasiphae to fall in sensual love with the bull. To please her wish, she made Daedalus, the fateful architect of the labyrinth, build her this enclave in order to copulate and give birth to the half-man, half bull which we know as the Minotaur.

34 HP, 61. HP-Godwin, 61.

35 Ibidem, 63. The original text is quite enjoyable. The reader can get the picture that Poliphilus was running as fast as he could!

36 As previously expressed in footnote n°28, Poliphilus is experiencing once again the "dark forest." And once again, he is also relieved when he finds himself in a pleasant realm of antiquarian inspiration and natural harmony.

CHAPTER 5

1 HP,92, HP-Godwin, 92-93.

2 For the purpose of this publication, I have included working sketches since the bridge's reconstruction are currently in progress. Ariani and Gabrielle (HP, 663-664) suggest that this bridge is a metaphor for the passage from one "barrier" or "dimension" to another, symbolizing the attainment of wisdom through every such passage (hence, the hieroglyphs). In this sense, Poliphilus is changing dimension from obscurity to wisdom and beauty. As an attempt to illustrate this metaphor, the artist re-constructions of the bridge will represent its immersion between the ruined pyramid (with obscure and thick vegetation), and the wide, fertile fields (leading towards the "realm" of Queen Eleutirillide).

3 The original inscription reads "*patientia est ornamentum custodia et protectio vitae.*" HP, 69, HP-Godwin, p. 69. For comments regarding hieroglyphs in the *Hypnerotomachia*, please refer to Chapter 1, note n° 3, P. 209.

4 "*…semper festina tarde…*" HP, 69.

5 HP, 77, HP-Godwin, 77.

6 It is most probable that "Eleutirillide" (along with her varied forms of presentation in the original text, "*Eleutirillida, Eleutirillyda, Eleuterillyde*") comes from the Greek work ελευθερία

*

(liberty). Mino and Gabrielle suggest in their comments that Eleutirillide is a symbol for "*liberalitas....[or that golden virtue known as love]...*" HP, 674.

7   This architectural term refers to the base on which structural columns rest upon. Also known as a "stylobate" or στιλοβατιζ. HP, 474.

8   For a more accurate description of the proportions and architecture of this building please refer to HP, 70-71 or HP-Godwin, 70. These descriptions along with my working sketches are an attempt to introduce the re-constructions currently under development.

9   It is interesting that Poliphilus refers to two terms used almost synonymously when it comes to ancient building materials: jasper is a type of chalcedony (a translucent variation of quartz originally from Asia Minor), mostly with green hues, considered by the ancients as a precious stone.

10 HP, 82. HP-Godwin, 82.

11 As Mino and Gabrielle clarify in their comments, Achoe comes from the Greek word ακοη, or "hearing." She accompanies Poliphilus along with Afea (αφη or "touch"), Osfressia (οσφρησια or "smell"), Orassia (ορασιζ or "sight"), and Geussia (γευσιζ or "taste"), all which are obviously symbolic for the senses. HP, 678.

12 The original woodcut showing this clever device includes the inscription ΓΕΛΟΙΑΣΤΟΣ, which means "to laugh." Ironically, Poliphilus could have been warned by the inscription the whole time, but obviously he was under the sensual influence of his lovely companions. Although the architectural representation is completely different from the Aldine text, the French baroque painter, Eustache Le Sueur captures this funny moment in one of his paintings (please refer to note n°1, Chapter 1, P. 209).

13 There are two pages in the *Hypnerotomachia* dedicated to Poliphilus' sexual game with his companions. HP, 86-87. HP-Godwin, 87.

14 In modern equivalents: 738 meters or 2,317 ft.

15 In modern equivalents: 9.14 meters, circa 28'-13" ft.

16 In modern equivalents: 88 meters, circa 276 ft. The courtyard itself has an area roughly of 7744 sq m. or 76,176 ft².

17 Please refer to Plate II of this Chapter, P. 120.

18 Comes from the Greek word αμεθνστος, which means "intoxicated by wine." Amethyst is a purple or violet sample of quartz.

19 Also known as "*antica verde*" or "*verd-antique*", this stone has a translucent quality, and green in colour occasionally doted with spots (similar to a serpent).

20 In modern equivalents: 12.4 cm or 6.4 English inches circa.

21 This is a type of decoration incorporating a continuous undulation of foliage.

22 Otherwise known as a husk.

23 In modern equivalents: 29.65 cm or 15 English inches.

24 In modern equivalents: 44.5 cm wide and 59.3 cm deep (1.4 ft wide and 1.9 ft deep).

25 In modern equivalents: 89 cm or 2.8 English feet.

26 HP, 91. HP-Godwin, 91.

27 Ibidem.

28 Ibidem.

29 For a hypothetical, artist re-construction of this finish, please refer to Plate VIII, of this Chapter, P. 126.

*

30   HP, 92, HP-Godwin, 91.

31   For a graphical layout of the main façade and plan, please refer to Plate I of this Chapter, P. 123.

32   According to commentaries by Mino and Gabrielle, these three curtains guarded by *Cinosia* (reason), *Indalomena* (imagination), and *Mnemosyna* (memory), symbolizes the three faculties or "ventricles" of the human mind, according to a classical reference that was already available in Medieval times (*"De Natura Hominis"* by Nemesius of Emesa). HP, 695.

33   HP, 94. HP-Godwin, 94. For a perspective view of this space, please refer to Plate XX of this chapter. For a plan and its dimensions, please refer to note n° 35, page 221.

34   In modern equivalents: 4.56 meters, circa 14'-4" ft.

35   HP, 94. HP-Godwin, 94-95. For clarity, the modern equivalents of these measurements are displayed in the following graph on P. 259.

36   Ibidem, see above for modern equivalents.

37   An elegant, deep-blue stone also used for preparing the pigment ultra-marine.

38   Also known as an architectural frieze.

39   "*...si articiosi, per quale arte, & temerario auso, & obstinato intento susseron cusi aptamente condicuti, o vero per glutino fabrile, o vero ferruminatione, o vero per malleatura, o vero per arte susoria. Per queste tre conditione di operare & fabrare il metallo, mi parue inpossibile, Che una copertura di tanta latitudine & nexo, fusse cusi optimamente fabricata...*" HP, 98. HP-Godwin, 98.

40   HP, p. 121-122. The original woodcut presented in the text illustrates these three doors in which Poliphilus must choose between "worldly greatness" (*gloria mundi*), fortune in love (*mater amoris*), and spiritual enlightenment (*gloria dei*). Being a loving fool as he is, Poliphilus chooses Love above spiritual or worldly greatness.

41   This precious stone has been identified by Mino and Gabriele as a type of diamond, symbolizing Poliphilus' new status as a "*...uomo libero...*" or free man. HP, 724.

42   Artist re-constructions for this garden are currently work in progress. I have included some of my concept sketches here in order to introduce the work. It is interesting to note that Mino and Gabriele have interpreted this garden as a symbol of Poliphilus' ascension from earthly existence, by pursuing a more "idealized" type of Love, alluded by the "ephemeral" quality of the glass construction described by our protagonist. HP, 727. A similar interpretation is presented by Kretzulesco-Quaranta: "*...La alegoría es transparente: ¿o no estamos en el Jardín de Vidrio? Los conscientes se dejan arrastrar al hilo de los sucesos de sus vidas, sucesos que no saben ni prever ni entender. Su experiencia terrenal terminará en una desintegración total. Para ellos no hay supervivencia...*" Kretzulesco-Quaranta, Emanuela, *Les Jardins du Songe. Poliphile et la Mystique de la Renaissance* (Paris, 1986), translated into the Spanish by Miguel Mingarro (Madrid, 1996), 162. As suggested by Poliphilus himself, similar workmanship found in this garden or "*viridiarium*" can be found today in examples of intricate, glass sculptures made by the legendary artisans on the island of Murano, in the Venetian Laguna, even to this day: "*...Perotosso,a,emte quivi la dulciloqua Logistica fece alquanta narratione, physiculabonda laudava la pæstante factione. & la nobilitate della material & arte & invento. (Quale non se trovarebbe in Muriano)...*" HP, 124. HP-Godwin, 124.

43   HP, 124. HP-Godwin, 124.

44   In the end, after Poliphilus' descriptions and with help of the original Aldine woodcuts, as well as those included in the French Edition by Jean Martin (Kerver, Paris, 1546), a complete series of artist re-constructions are currently underway.

*

45 Mino and Gabriele, HP, 728. Their comments were interestingly informative: In medieval iconography, the tower, as an archetype, is perceived as a symbol of "over-seeing" intelligence. For a graphical re-construction, please refer to Plates XXVII and XXVIII of this Chapter, pages 145-146.

46 It is interesting to note that the number seven (either in divided combinations or a complete set) appears quite often in Poliphilus' descriptions. According to Mino & Gabriele, the meaning of this garden refers to the Planetary Orbits, and how they can influence human destiny through the various passages of life: "...la conformazione planetaria del labirinto...è essenziale per farne un simbolo della vita e del tempo che tutto divora..." HP, 728.

47 A graphical reconstruction can be seen on Plates XXIII-XXVII of this Chapter, pages 141-145.

48 Another wise description is inscribed in the entrance of the first tower of the labyrinth: ΔΟΖΑ ΚΟΣΜΙΚΗΟΣ ΓΟΜΦΟΛΙΣ: "...le glorie del mondo sono bolle d'aria..." Mino and Gabriele, HP, 144. My translation is: "all the glory of the world is nothing but bubbles in the air."

49 HP, 126. HP-Godwin, 126.

50 "...beato chi raggiunge la metà..." Mino and Gabriele, HP, 145. The curators suggest in their commentaries, that this point is the first time a person stops to look back at what they have done, and to surpass the anxiety caused by perceiving how time moves so quickly at an adult age: "...La sorte universale della quinta stazione marziana...soccorre I naviganti nel superare le avversità dell'età adulta e della prima, angosciosa percezione della fuga del tempo..." HP, 739.

51 HP-Godwin, 126. Poliphilus' original description is clear: "...Ove cum sincero examine il medio si discerne cum chi se ha coniugato la fœlicitate, o beatitudine dingengo, o vero di copia. La quale non seco havendola, negli sequenti meno quasi valeno acquistare..." HP, 126.

52 Ibidem.

53 Ibidem.

54 Kretzulesco-Quaranta has a very interesting explanation for this "device" linking it to the ideas proposed by Cardenal Niccola di Cusa, who was an active member of the Accademia under Pope Nicolas V. His theories of geometrical reduction arriving at a perfect circle (or "search for knowledge"), are very similar to the objectives of this monumental expression: "...la iluminación de todas las cosas creadas; su gobierno, y la bondad divina – la caridad – abrazando el todo..." In addition, Kretzulesco gives an interesting suggestion that this numerical and geometrical matrix of divine representation introduced by Niccola di Cusa was probably of Asian influence (through the Chinese "law if cycles"). Kretzulesco-Quaranta, Emanuela, Les Jardins du Songe. Poliphile et la Mystique de la Renaissance (Paris, 1986), translated into the Spanish by Miguel Mingarro (Madrid, 1996), 164-165.

55 The term areostyle and the type of arrangement mentioned by Vitruvius in his treatise (referring to wider spaces between intercolumniation, including pediments in the Tuscan fashion, and the use of gilded bronze statues, etc.) is very familiar to architectural characteristics described by Poliphilus when referring to the "displuvio" at this point in his tale. Vitruvius states: "...species autem aedium sunt quinque, quarum ea sunt vocabula:...spatiis intercolumniorum, diastylos amplius quam oportet patentibus, rare inter se didcutis araeostylos...In araeostylos autem nec lapideis nec marmoreis epistyliis uti datur, sed inpondendae de materia traves perpetuae. Et ipsarum aedium species sunt varicae, barycephalae, humiles, latae, ornanturque sognis fictilibus aut aereis inauratis eari, fasogoa tuscanico more, uti est ad Circum Maximus Cereis et Herculis Pompaeiani, item Capitolii..." Marcus Vitruvius Polio, De Architectura Libri X – Edizioni Studio Tesi, Traduzione di Luciano Migotto (Padova, 1990), 135.

*

<u>Modern equivalents:</u>
28 paces = 41 meters, 128.70 ft. * 3 paces = circa 17 meters, 53.4 ft.

1 pace = circa 7 meters, 22 ft. * 8 squares x 3 piedi = 5 meters, 16 ft.

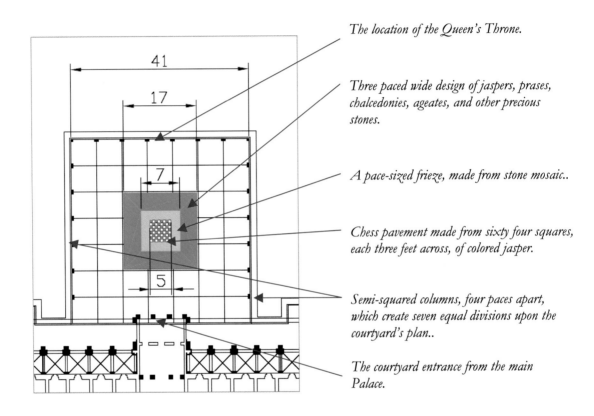

The location of the Queen's Throne.

Three paced wide design of jaspers, prases, chalcedonies, ageates, and other precious stones.

A pace-sized frieze, made from stone mosaic..

Chess pavement made from sixty four squares, each three feet across, of colored jasper.

Semi-squared columns, four paces apart, which create seven equal divisions upon the courtyard's plan..

The courtyard entrance from the main Palace.

47. ENDNOTE N°35 OF CHAPTER 6: THE QUEEN'S THRONE COURTYARD DESCRIBED BY POLIPHILUS.

*

56   HP-Godwin, 128. In the original Aldine text: "…*in questo medio centrico mysteriosamente era fundata una basi di diaphano Calcedonio in forma cubica…*" HP, 128.

57   In modern equivalents: 60 cm high and 2.23 m in diameter (1.9 ft high and 7 ft in diameter).

58   Ibidem, 129. In the original Aldine edition: "…*DIVINAE INFINITAEQUE TRINITATI UNIUS ESSENTIAE…*" HP, 129. According to Mino and Gabriele, this monument has no historical, archaeological, or literary precedent, and therefore, describes it as a true mystery. For a detailed analysis of this object, please refer to their commentaries for this section. HP, 747-761.

59   According to Mino and Gabriele, each face of the three sphinxes (first a human, second a beast, and a third, part-human and part beast) is evident in the Platonic view of the sub-divisions of the human spirit: "…*Come spiega ancora Platone l'anima simboleggiandone con la parte umana la sua razionalità, con quella leonine la sua natura irascibile, con quella policefala, per la pluralità dei suoi aspetti, la sua natura concupiscibile: la figura umana, la razionalità, primeggia di gran lunga sulla figura leonine…in quanto la 'virtue' si realizza quando l'uomo sa sottomettere la propria parte animalesca a quella razionale. Il Colonna…segue questa gerarchia trinitaria…*" HP, 754.

60   HP-Godwin, 130.

61   Ibidem.

62   Ibidem. As a conclusion, this monument intertwines the following entities into one existence: (1) Time (past present and future represented by the Greek letters O, N, Ω on the three faces of the golden obelisk), (2) the Human Soul (represented by the three creatures that sustain the golden obelisk), (3) Love (the fire glyph), (4) God (the sun glyph), (5) Wisdom (the rudder glyph), and (6) the cubic base of translucent chalcedony, which remains a mystery, until "*quantunue instructissimi, non hano pero atro acquisito, che el fe vide…*" HP, 130.

CHAPTER 6

1   HP, 206. HP-Godwin, 204.

2   *Physizoa* or *Genetrix* (in Latin), refers to the "creator" or "mother Earth". According to Ariani and Gabriele, the inspiration probably comes from the a classical reference: Julius Caesar's famous temple dedicated to Venus Genetrix mentioned by Pliny and Suetonius, among others. HP, 835.

3   HP, 196-197. HP-Godwin, 196-197.

4   Ibidem.

5   Modern equivalent: 60 cm circa, 1.9 English feet.

6   HP, 837. As Ariani and Gabriele point out, the height of the Ionic column (equivalent to nine times the thickness of its base) is an allegory directly from Alberti. L.B Alberti, *L'Architettura* (Milano, 1989), 302-303.

7   A similar solution can be seen in the circular plan of the Church of Santo Stefano Rotondo in Rome (5th century AD), restored by Nicholas V (the "humanist Pope"), in 1453.

8   This material refers to metal work that comes from the Po river valley (ex-Bononia Galliae), or as Roman geography calls "Gallia Cisalpina", mentioned by Alberti. HP, 839. In Godwin's translation, the word "glass" is used to simplify the Italian word "*lamine,*" which literary means "membrane" or "a thin foil or leaf (of metal)", which is more a biological or chemical definition than an architectural one.

9   Petosiris and Necepso were mythical astrologists from ancient Egypt who were famed during medieval and Renaissance times. HP, 840.

10   HP, 200. HP-Godwin, 200.

11   Ibidem, 207.

NOTES

*

12 The ancient city of Pergamum was located in Mysia, Asia Minor, and was famous for its school of sculpture, which flourished there during the III and II centuries B.C.E. This explains an error on the part of the author of the *Hypnerotomachia* when mentioning Zenodorus, which was not a mosaic artist, but was instead a famous sculptor. HP, 849.

13 As Ariani and Gabriele point out in detail, the original Aldine text ("...*il litostrato in Praeneste nel delubro dilla Fortuna*) quotes directly from Pliny's description (and choice of terminology) for the mosaics found in what used to be this temple (located circa 60 km east of Rome): "...*Lithostrota...quod in Fortunae delubro Praeneste...*" The term "lithostrota" is a classical, architectural term referring to mosaic work made from very tiny stone pieces. HP, 849.

14 Ibidem, 201.

15 Ibidem, 203.

16 Ibidem.

17 HP, 210. HP-Godwin, 209.

18 HP, 210. HP-Godwin, 210.

19 This is the crescent moon dominated by an eagle. As Mino and Gabriele point out, this iconographic architectural combination has connection with recognizing the classical past, in particular, ancient Rome: the moon, which symbolizes antiquarian significance to ancient Roman monuments (the Colosseum, Trajan's Column, etc.). The eagle is identified with Jupiter, or the father of the cosmos. The curators also interestingly point out that Andrea Mantegna incorporates this architectural iconography in his "Triumphs of Caesar" to mysteriously glorify the Roman, antiquarian past. HP, 852.

20 As Mino and Gabriele point out, this term comes from Κυλλον πηρα, which refers to the Greek name of the sanctuary dedicated to Aphrodite (Goddess of Love) on Mount Imeto. It was known that the water from this monument's ceremonial fountain recovered fertile qualities to sterile women, which gives significance to the regenerative nature of Venus, the Mother Creator (or Physizoa, whose temple this is dedicated to). HP, 854-855.

21 HP-Godwin, 212.

22 This of course is Polia, Poliphilus' re-found lover. HP, 214. HP-Godwin, 213.

CHAPTER 7

1 HP, 242. HP-Godwin, 242.

2 Ibidem.

3 For a better understanding of the Polyandrion's re-construction with the elements described in the following paragraphs, please refer to "Plate I – Plan and Elevation of the Polyandrion", P. 195.

4 Numidian stone, or otherwise known as *Giallo Antico*, is a light, yellowish marble used in Roman times, which originally comes from North Africa. Hymettian stone is a grey-bluish marble, while Laconic or "Spartan" marble is also known as *verde porfido*, which is a deep green marble with white, crystal spots. For a graphical understanding regarding the aesthetics of these classical marbles, please refer to "Plate IX – Plate X" of this Chapter, P. 203-204.

5 This obviously is red Theban granite, from ancient Egypt, which is the same material used for the obelisk for the Great Pyramid's summit (Chapter 2). For a graphical understanding of this stone, please refer to "Plate XII – Materials: Red Theban Granite" of this Chapter, P. 206.

6 The original Aldine edition reads: "...*Iustitia recta amicitia et odio evaginata et nuda. Et ponderata liberalitas regnum firmiter servat...*" HP, 243. HP-Godwin, 243.

7 "...*DIVO IULIO CAESARI SEMP. AUG. TOTIUS ORB. GUBERNAT. OB ANIMI*

*

CLEMENTE. ET LIBERALITATEMA AEGYPTII COMMUNIA ERE.S.EREXERE..." HP, 244. HP-Godwin, 244.

8 "...PACE, ACCONCORDIA PARVAER ESCRESCUNT, DISCORDIA MAXIMA EDECRESCUNT..." Ibidem.

9 "...MILITARIS PRUDENTIA, SEU DISCIPLINA IMPERII EST TENACISSIMUM VINCULUM..." Ibidem, 245.

10 "...DIVI IULII VICTORIA ARUMET SPOLIORUM COPIOSISSIMUM TROPHAEUM, SEU INSIGNIA..." Ibidem.

11 "...D.M.S. CADAVERIB. AMORE FURENTIUM MISERABUNDIS POLYANDRION..." Ibidem, 246. My translation: "Consecrated to the hands of the Gods, this Cemetery for those miserable corpses who were maddened by Love."

12 Ibidem.

13 A graphical understanding of this material and archetype can be found in "Plate XI – Materials: Ciborium" of this Chapter, P. 276.

14 HP, 248. HP-Godwin, 248.

15 For the purpose of this publication, my artist re-constructions show this temple complex in tact, not withstanding Poliphilus' description indicating their horrible state of conservation. The reason being is that it was necessary to understand the relation ship between the circular, roofless temple in relation to the Ciborium, the surrounding Tribuna, and the "Egyptian" obelisk dedicated to Julius Caesar. The resulting rendering re-constructions are found on pages 195-206 of the Plates section of this chapter. The hypogeum below the ciborium is currently in design phase.

16 A highly porous volcanic stone used by the Romans for heavy foundation and rustification work. Examples of this type of construction with tufa stone can be seen today in Rome, in an area, for example, in what used to be a part of Augustus' Forum near Trajan's Market (today in Via Tor de' Conti).

17 HP, 249. HP-Godwin, 249.

18 HP, 250. HP-Godwin, 250.

19 "D. M." is a Roman funerary expression referring "to the hands of the gods", or as Godwin translates, "...to the blessed shades..." HP-Godwin, 469.

20 A couple sadly dedicate this epitaph to their little daughter of divine and loving inspiration, who died very young.

21 This mysterious set of images includes the following inscription that reads: "Have Leria omnia amantissima. Valè", or as Godwin translates, "Hail, Leria, most beloved of all, farewell." HP-Godwin, 469. Ariani and Gabriele were able to find a literary precedent that goes back to Virgil. However, they do point out that the "Bacchus-like" quality of the iconography incised in the epigraph, probably alludes to amorous and orgiastic rites dedicated to Dionysus (Bacchus), celebrating the memory to this lover. HP, 923-924.

22 The inscription reads (in modern Italian) "...cenere dei morti...niente è più certo della morte..." HP, 264. My translation: "...ashes of the deceased...nothing is more certain than Death..."

23 This heart-wrenching story is well translated by Godwin, HP-Godwin, 469-470.

24 There are many other epitaphs that Poliphilus discovers in the cemetery near the temple complex. HP-Godwin, 469-471. Currently, the artist re-constructions that represent this part of the cemetery and its various epitaphs are in design phase.

25 My translation (from the modern Italian): "Ashes of Queen Artemisia (of Caria)", HP, 271.

NOTES

*

26 "…ΕΡΟΤΟΣ ΚΑΤΟΓΤΡΟΝ…" which means "mirror of love". HP, 266.

27 HP, 270. HP-Godwin, 270.

28 Ibidem, 272.

BIBLIOGRAPHY

*

PRIMARY SOURCES

EDITIONS OF THE *HYPNEROTOMACHIA POLIPHILI*:

Colonna, F. *Hypnerotomachia Poliphili, Venetiis, in aedibus Aldi Mantii.* Venice, 1499.

Colonna, F. *Hypnerotomachia Poliphili,* introduction and comments by G. Pozzi and L.A. Ciapponi. Vol. I-II. Padua, 1980.

Colonna, F. *Hypnerotomachia Poliphili,* translation into the Italian and comments by Marco Ariani and Mino Gabriele. Vol. I-II. Milan, 1998.

Colonna, F. *Le Songe de Poliphile*, translation into the French by Jean Martin (Paris, Kerver, 1546), presentation, transliteration, notes, glossary, and index by Gilles Polizzi. Paris, 1994.

Colonna, F. *Hypnerotomachia. The Strife of Love in a Dreame* (London, 1592), translated into the English by R.D., a facsimile reproduction of the Longleat copy and introduction by Lucy Gent. London, 1973.

Colonna, F. *Hypnerotomachia Poliphili: The Strife of Love in a Dream,* translation and introduction by Joscelyn Godwin. London and New York, 1999.

Colonna, F. *Sueño de Polífilo*, introduction, translation, and comments in the Spanish by Pilar Pedraza. Barcelona, 1999.

EDITIONS OF ARCHITECTURAL TREATIES AND ANTIQUARIANISM:

Agustinus, A. *Diálogos de medallas, inscriciones y otras antigüidades.* Madrid, 1744.

Alberti, L.B. *L'architettura - De Re Aedificatoria,* translation in the Italian by Giovanni Orlandi with comments and notes by Paolo Portoghesi. Milan, 1989.

Alberti, L.B. *On the Art of Building in Ten Books,* translated by Joseph Rykwert, Neil Leach and Robert Tavernor. Cambridge, 1999.

Ficacci, L. *Giovanni Battista Piranesi, The Complete Etchings. Istituto Nazionale per la Grafica di Roma.* Cologne, 2000.

Orapollo. *I Geroglifici*, introduzione, traduzione e note di Mario Andrea Rigoni e Elena Zanco. Milan, 1996.

Polio, Marcus Vitruvius. *De Architectura Libri X,* translation in the Italian by Luciano Migotto. Padova, 1990

Serlio, S. *Architettura di Sebastiano Serlio Bolognese, in sei libri divisa. Ne quali vengono dottamente, & con ogni chiarezza spiegate tutte le oscurità, & secreti dell'Arte. Nuovamente impressi in beneficio universale in Lingua Latina, & Volgare, con alcune aggiunte.* Venice, 1663.

OTHER SOURCES:

Borsi, S. *Polifilo architetto: Cultura architettonica e teoria artistica nell'Hypnerotomachia Poliphili di Francesco Colonna, 1499.* Rome, 1995.

Calvesi, M. *La "pugna d'amore in sogno" di Francesco Colonna romano.* Rome, 1996.

Calvesi, M. *Il Sogno di Polifilo prenestino.* Rome, 1980.

Kretzulesco-Quaranta, E. *Les Jardins du Songe. Poliphile et la Mystique de la Renaissance* (Paris, 1986), translated into the Spanish by Miguel Mingarro. Madrid, 1996.

Lefaivre, L. *Leon Battista Alberti's Hypnerotomachia Poliphili: Re-Cognizing the Architectural Body in the Early Italian Renaissance.* Cambridge, 1996.

Meogrossi, P. *L'Hypnerotomachia Poliphili, un racconto antiquario per il Palatino.* Annexe, Ac.Française, Rome, pp. 227-238.

Schmeiser, L. *Das Werk des Druckers: Untersuchengen zum buch Hypnerotomachia Poliphili.* Vienna, 2003.

BIBLIOGRAPHY

*

White, I. *The Architecture in Poliphilo's Dream,* Octavo's Edition of the *Hypnerotomachia Poliphili* from the Lessing J. Rosenwald collection, U.S. Library of Congress. Oakland, 2004.

RENAISSANCE CULTURE AND THE BUILDING ARTS:

Furnari, M. *Formal Design in Renaissance Architecture from Brunelleschi to Palladio.* New York, 1995.

Mosser, M. and Teyssot, G. *L'architettura dei giardini d'Occidente dal Rinascimento al Novecento.* Milan, 1990.

Murray, P. *The Architecture of the Italian Renaissance.* London, 1963.

Visentini, M. A. *La Villa in Italia: Quattrocento e Cinquecento.* Milan, 1995.

CLASSICAL ANTIQUITY AND THE BUILDING ARTS:

Connolly, P. *The Ancient City: Life in Classical Athens and Rome.* Oxford, 1998.

Grimal, P. *I giardini di Roma antica.* Milano, 1990.

Mannucci, V. *Atlante di Ostia antica.* Venice, 1995.

Marino, L. *Dizionario di Restauro Archeologico.* Firenze, 2003.

Marta, R. *Tecnica costruttiva romana.* Rome, 1991.

Matini, M. L. M. *Mosaici antichi in Italia: Regione Prima – Roma, Reg. X Palatium,* dell'Istituto Poligrafico dello Stato. Rome, 1967.

Novelli, I.. *Atlas of Rome: The Form of the City on a 1:1000 Scale Photomap and Line Map.* Venice, 1992.

Stierlin, H. *Impero Romano: Dagli etruschi alla caduta dell'Impero Romano.* Cologne, 1997.

Smith, T. G. *Vitruvius on Architecture.* New York, 2003.

SECONDARY SOURCES

Fogliati, S and Dutto, D. *Il Giardino di Polifilo: ricostruzione virtuale dalla Hypnerotomachia Poliphili di Francesco Colonna stampata a Venezia nel 1499 da Aldo Manuzio.* Milan, 2002.

Gombrich, E. H. *Immagini simboliche: Studi sull'arte nel Rinascimento.* Turin, 1978.

Grafton, A. *Leon Battista Alberti: Master Builder of the Italian Renaissance.* Cambridge, 2000.

Kluckert, E. *Giardini d'Europa: Dall'antichità oggi.* Cologne, 2000.

Kruft, H. *Geschichte der Architekturetheorie: Von der Antike bis zur Gegenwart* (Munich, 1985), translated into the English by Ronald Taylor Elsie Callander, and Antony Wood. New York, 1994.

Millon, H. A. and Lampugnani, V. M. *The Renaissance from Brunelleschi to Michelangelo : The Representation of Architecture.* New York, 1997.

Pastorello, E. *Di Aldo Manuzio: Testimonianze e Documenti.* Florence, 1965.

Pérez-Gómez, A. *Polyphilo or the Dark Forest Revisited: An Erotic Epiphany of Architecture.* Cambridge, 1992.

Tafuri, M. *Venezia e il Rinascimento.* Turin, 1985.

Tzonis, A. and Lefaivre, L. *Classical Architecture: The Poetics of Order.* Cambridge, 1986.

Valsecchi, F. *Incunaboli dell'ambrosiana.* Vicenza, 1972.

Vasari, G. *Le Vite de' più eccelenti pittori scultori architettori nella redazione del 1550 e 1560,* Vol. I-IV, curate by Rosanna Bettarini, with secular comments by Paola Barocchi. Florence, 1927.

ABOUT THE AUTHOR

*

Esteban Cruz has a degree in architecture from the California Polytechnic State University in San Luis Obispo, with post-graduate studies at the *Istituto Universitario di Architettura Venezia* (IUAV) in Venice, Italy. Since 1996, he has worked on projects in the fields of architecture, urban planning, and conservation, and is currently project manager for an Italian-American firm in Milan engaged primarily in international practice.

His interest in history and computers started in 1998 as design consultant for the development of a prototype virtual museum (N.u.M.E.), for the historic city center of Bologna, Italy. Coordinated by the University of Bologna, this project involved historic re-constructions of important monumental areas of the city from the XII to the XVII centuries. It was displayed for the first time at the international conference of IT and computer innovation, SIGGRAPH 1999 in Los Angeles. This and other contributions to the fields of Historic and Cultural Heritage, has lead Esteban to be an active member of the International Council of Museums (ICOM).

His interest and research activities dealing with the *Hypnerotomachia Poliphili* began in 1995 while still as an undergraduate. Since then, he is continuously active in developing graphical reconstructions that "illustrate" the architecture and landscapes encrypted in this Renaissance text.

Esteban is an associate member of both the American Institute of Architects (AIA) and the Royal Institute of the Architects of Ireland (RIAI). He is married and lives between San Francisco, California and Milan, Italy.

ISBN 141205324-2

◆

Edwards Brothers Malloy
Ann Arbor MI. USA
July 13, 2017